RELIGIOUS DIAGNOSIS IN A SECULAR SOCIETY

A Staff for the Journey

Donald D. Denton, Jr.

University Press of America,® Inc.
Lanham • New York • Oxford

Copyright © 1998 by
University Press of America,® Inc.
4720 Boston Way
Lanham, Maryland 20706

12 Hid's Copse Rd.
Cummor Hill, Oxford OX2 9JJ

Library of Congress Cataloging-in-Publication Data

Denton, Donald D.
Religious diagnosis in a secular society : a staff for the journey /
Donald D. Denton, Jr.
p.   cm.
Includes bibliographical references and index.
1. Pastoral pyschology. 2. Psychodiagnostics. I. Title.
BV4012.D368   1997   253.5'2—DC21   97-41784 CIP

ISBN 0-7618-0965-1 (pbk: alk. ppr.)

⊖™ The paper used in this publication meets the minimum
requirements of American National Standard for information
Sciences—Permanence of Paper for Printed Library Materials,
ANSI Z39.48—1984

Dedication

To my great-grandfather, Alvin B. Rice whose walking stick provided
the inspiration,
and
William B. Oglesby, Jr., whose integration of the language of the Bible
with the language of the clinic
provided the model.

Table of Contents

Foreword

Most clinical and scientific progress occurs gradually as thinkers evolve ideas. Once in a great while a step change will occur. A book or article will advance the clinical field greatly. Don Denton has offered such a book.

I have been involved in clinical work with Christians for over twenty years. In that time, I have studied the research and contributed to scholarship on religious diagnosis and treatment. Yet I have always been quite dissatisfied with religious diagnosis. Browning, Pruyser, and Malony have offered systems of religious diagnosis that are quite complete and useful for pastoral counseling. Researchers have created numerous scales to measure aspects of religiosity (see Hill & Benner, 1998, who have collected enough instruments to fill two volumes). Yet, there is little agreement about which scales and psychometric methods are most useful. At one series of three conferences on religion and spirituality that took place in 1996 and 1997, some of the best thinkers in the field of the scientific study of religion arrived at what I would call the minimalist position, that religious assessment could be done by using three items--one to measure attendance at religious services, one to measure religious commitment, and one to measure spiritual commitment. While using the minimalist religious assessment strategy might enhance the scientific investigation of religion--principally because the state of the field is at such an impoverished state of development--the system of religious assesment is not very illuminating in the clinic and would hardly satisfy even a secular clinician whose client had a strong religious value system.

Don Denton has provided an alternative approach to religious assessment. The approach is loosely modeled on the concept of independent "axes" used by the Diagnostic and Statistical Manual of the American Psychiatric Association (4th edition) for diagnosing mental disorders (DSM-IV). The axes for religious assessment are ethical guilt (Axis I), covenantal betrayal (Axis II), and existential defilement (Axis III). These represent three levels of involvement with evil and sin.

For example, take a person who seeks therapy because he is depressed at having discovered he is HIV positive. Although the man is married, he has had numerous affairs over the last several years. In one of those, he contracted HIV virus. He claims to be a Christian, yet feels compelled to enter illicit sexual relationships. Investigation reveals no early traumas, such as physical or sexual abuse. The person might be diagnosed on the DSM-IV as having Major Depression (Axis I), traits of an Obsessive-Compulsive Personality Disorder (Axis II), HIV-positive medical diagnosis (Axis III), no interaction with social systems (Axis IV), and a GAF of 50 (suicidal ideation; Axis V). What is this person's religious diagnosis?

Calling him a sinner isn't very illuminating (though it is correct). Describing him as being a once-per-week church attender, committed moderately to his Protestant Christian religion, and committed moderately to his spirituality are also true but not particularly helpful to the clinician.

With Denton's system, though, the person could be described as having a number of Axis I religious difficulties. He has ethical and moral difficulties of being unfaithful. He feels intense guilt over his sinful sexual encounters, his secrecy from his wife, his unwillingness to tell her that he is HIV positive, and his inability to control his actions. He also feels guilty over his lukewarm religious and spiritual commitment.

His Axis II religious diagnosis (covenantal betrayal) suggests five major covenant betrayals. He has most obviously violated the marriage covenant through his unfaithful sexual behavior and his romantic attractions to various illicit lovers. Second, he has violated the Christian covenant to be faithful to God and to accept the reliance on God that his Christian understanding makes appropriate for him. Third, he has violated a covenant of connection to the church, as he has removed himself from a community of people to whom he feels accountability. The covenantal betrayals also cut the other way. Fourth, he feels betrayed by his sexual partner who infected him with the HIV virus. Fifth, upon further exploration, he even feels that God has violated an implicit covenant with him. He feels, even though he states he knows intellectually that this feeling is not correct, that God owed him health because of his years of adherence to Christianity.

His Axis III religious diagnosis (defilement) is his profound sense of abandonment that he currently experiences and that he anticipates when he reveals--if he reveals--his serostatus to his wife. He fears that his family, friends, co-workers, and even acquaintances will abandon him and treat him as a pariah. He sees his potential revelation of his serostatus as an altruistic act that will require great sacrifice and will have great cost.

In Denton's diagnostic system, the clinician is left with a plan for action to help the person with his religious issues. At the level of Axis I, the clinician can listen to the unfolding story of guilt and shame with empathy and love. The clinician can help the man process his guilt feelings, admit his sin, seek forgiveness, and pursue reconciliation with God. The clinician can help the man deal with his confession to his wife and the fallout that happens after that revelation. At the level of Axis II, the clinician can help the man grieve over the violations of covenant he has done and he has perceived to have happened to him. The man can encounter the evil and unfaithfulness in people's hearts--including (if therapy is successful) in his own. He can pursue forgiveness and extend forgiveness in humility. At the level of Axis III, the clinician can help restore the man through promoting reconciliation and reattachment. At the profound level of the experience of abandonment, the man probably feels alienated from humanity. The clinician's task is to help the man feel less of an alien and more connection.

True religion reaches through the skin, beyond the heart, into the soul of the person, and then to the soul's connection with God. I think Denton has added substantially to our ability to describe more fully the ways that religion penetrates the person's skin, permeates the person, and reaches the Divine-human relationship. In a way, Denton's system helps the clinician think *humanly* about diagnosis. It moves clinicians beyond their role as "clinician" and helps them consider the person sitting across from them. I suspect that not merely diagnosis but also human interaction will benefit when one uses Denton's approach.

Everett L. Worthington, Jr.
Richmond, Virginia
July, 1997

Preface

These are difficult times for all who provide human care. Increasingly complex medical procedures produce miraculous cures of the body but may bankrupt the patient. Psychotropic drugs now stabilize people to lead productive lives instead of warehousing them in large, forbidding facilities. But the primary cost of such advances appears to be in the area of our human soul.

The editor of *The American Journal of Psychiatry* recently noted "changes in health care are placing us under increasing pressure to become only physicians of the body and to abandon our responsibilities for the mind and soul (Psychiatry 153:5: 589). Significantly, a professor of pastoral care at a noted seminary recently recalled being asked "what do you have to say about this case that the psychologist and social worker haven't already said?" (Townsend 1996:349). When those who care for the mind and the soul agree on the loss of humane focus in the care of human beings, it is an indication of the depth and breadth of our distress. This distress has many causes, not the least of which is the pressure to deliver care fast, inexpensively and simply. This pressure comes from a variety of sources, but those who sit with and care for hurting people feel frustrated by the pressure.

A part of the difficulty that clinicians and providers of mental health care face is the loss of a shared language or system to speak about those dynamics which are the most personal. We are too sophisticated to use a concept like "soul," in spite of Dr. Andreasen's perceptive remarks. Religiously oriented counselors and pastors are too unsure of our special contribution as professionals in spite of a clinical training movement that is over fifty years old. What can be done, theoretically and practically, to redress this loss? Can we find our way out of this dilemma?

I believe a significant part of our dilemma can be resolved if we begin to agree on a shared diagnostic language. Clinically trained pastoral counselors and religiously oriented mental health practitioners already use the DSM-IV with as much competence as psychiatrists. What is needed is a common schema for speaking about religious, spiritual matters. We have to find a pattern that respects the diversity of religious viewpoints, pieties and theologies in our pluralistic society without becoming so unwieldly that it obstructs the clinical process.

We also have to encourage caregivers, whether religious or secular, to include such material in their case notes, clinical consultations and insurance claim write-ups even if there is at first resistance to including such non-verifiable material in a supposedly "facts only" world.

The system I propose in this volume works in the clinical setting. I use it and teach it to chaplains, pastors, social workers and other clinicians. I include it in forms filed with insurance companies, on case write-ups to other professionals and to the court system. I find that when we bring a person's spirituality into the counseling process, explicitly, we deepen our connection with that person in a responsible, respectful fashion. By reminding ourselves and third-parties about this dimension of the person we accomplish a profound, but little reported change in the counseling process. We begin to recover a sense of the holiness of the person. The recovery of these spiritual values may go to restoring a recognition of the sacredness of the relationship between caregiver and hurting person. If we can accomplish this, we may proceed a ways toward producing healing, not only for those who receive our care but also for a health care system that all too often fails to exhibit genuine care.

Donald D. Denton, Jr., D. Min., L. P. C.
Pentecost, 1997

Acknowledgments

Dr. Paul Pruyser was the keynote speaker at the first regional meeting of the American Association of Pastoral Counselors which I attended. His remarks and writings have been guides in my service as a pastor and counselor. I would be remiss not to note his influence on my work.

The A.A.P.C. *Working Group on Pastoral Diagnosis,* my colleagues and students at the Virginia Institute of Pastoral Care and at Hunter-Holmes McGuire Veterans Hospital in Richmond, Virginia, have provided encouragement and critique throughout the process of clinical trials and manuscript preparation. Dr. Mary Fran Hughes-McIntyre, Director of Education, deserves special mention for her thoughtful, careful critique.

Dr. Everett Worthington of Virginia Commonwealth University, has written a thoughtful and perceptive foreword. Dr. William Arnold of Union Theological Seminary in Virginia, Dr. Dan Bagby of Baptist Theological School in Richmond, Dr. Gwen Hawley of the Presbyterian School of Christian Education and Dr. John Kinney of the School of Theology at Virginia Union University each reviewed the manuscript and made helpful suggestions.

Several congregations have reminded me of the power of the local church to be places of care: LaSalle Street Church, Ravenswood Presbyterian, Lincoln Park Presbyterian , Cutler Presbyterian, Beulah Presbyterian and Brett-Reed Presbyterian churches deserve special mention.

Several people along the way have shaped my skill as a writer and researcher. Though some have not lived to see this volume published, their names should not be forgotten: Doris Rothelisberger, Evangeline Bell, James Ashbrook.

The individuals whose lives have trusted me to journey with them in their search for care and cure continue to inspire me. Although their names and circumstances have been altered in this volume, their names and faces remain in my heart.

Introduction
Patterns of Religious Diagnosis

Father and son came together to the pastor's office. The tall young man looked sad and frightened. His father's face bore the marks of a sleepless night. A detective had visited them the prior afternoon, laying before the family the charges of molestation brought against the son by a younger neighbor boy.

"My life is in the toilet!" came the son's pithy evaluation of his condition.

"It may not be," replied the father. "That's why we're here, to see how you can salvage your life and we can all understand the pain you could not express any other way."

Long before we gathered around the smoke wafting from the cigar of Sigmund Freud, we have drawn close to the warmth of council fires to seek healing. Whether we called them a priest, shaman, *curandero*, or monk, we came with the expectation that this representative of the gods would both understand our pain and be an agent of healing. Regardless of the public myth about how the healer restored our health, we know that their practice was based upon a system of diagnosis which guided treatment.

Our understanding of disease and health has advanced. The technology currently available for the healing of our bodies is breathtaking. Yet the deeper burdens of the human condition remain fundamentally unchanged. These burdens may result from illness and lead us into physical disease. Our burdens may also result from the human condition. The source does not matter. Persons still gather near the warmth of another human to find healing for the ache of loneliness, the sadness of grief, the confusion of incest and the mysteries of our dreams. Methods for understanding the nature of these ailments as well as directing our care of others can be very complex or very simple. All seem to have some efficacy for some persons.

The Purpose of Diagnosis

Diagnostic frameworks serve the dual purpose of naming the pain and directing the care. While one may debate the efficacy of a particular framework for a specific situation, one encounters such frameworks in whatever culture one cares to examine. Medieval culture utilized the Seven Deadly Sins and the writings of Gregory the Great to accomplish these tasks.[1] A rich variety of cultures utilize ways of diagnosis that seem initially foreign to our understanding but describe very recognizable human anguish. They too guide the caregiver in producing health.[2] There is a diversity within our own small slice of modern religious life. Within the author's city a client may receive quality pastoral care from a professional who utilizes the DSM-IV to guide her interventions, supplemented by the use of psychological testing. One may also receive care from one who uses Biblical stories to understand the nature of his clients' distress.

Such diversity in diagnosis and care is not limited to the religious community. Although the DSM-IV has standardized the current universe of diagnosis, clinicians still routinely ask one another, "is this the real diagnosis or is it the *insurance* diagnosis?" Treatment for an agreed-upon diagnosis is likewise diverse, in spite of the pressures of managed care. Various clinicians may write a treatment plan that looks remarkably uniform but their actual practice will vary significantly. Secular clinicians are increasingly aware that spiritual values must be included even in brief therapy.[3]

The efficacy of religious care, quite apart from formal therapy by a religiously oriented clinician, is increasingly recognized by secular agencies. The DSM-IV now recognizes Religious or Spiritual Problem as a specific diagnosis (DSM-IV, 685). The various 12-Step recovery programs that address a variety of human problems, while maintaining a religiously neutral stance, nevertheless encourage a *de facto* religious consciousness through the imagery of the Higher Power. Thus it is common for the average parish pastor to have within a congregation at least one person who has had experience with the therapeutic use of religious imagery. It is also common for secular therapists to be treating people being assisted by one of these 12-Step programs.

Religious caregivers have known for millennia that appearances of health are deceptive. Quite apart from the formal structures of disease and care, persons wrestle with events and feelings which try our patience, pocketbook and perspicuity. Sudden tragedies place us in desperate straits. A spouse's winning lottery ticket transforms our future. The tremor of the earth can shatter a lifetime of work and dreams. Saying farewell to our final child reminds us of our own approaching *adieu* to this world. These are not problems that cry out for a solution. They are the universal marks of our human condition. But these are a few of the multitude of situations which bring people to the religious community for praise, prayer, soothing and celebration.

Such events surely affect our *awareness of the Holy*[4] as well as tugging at what Don Browning so aptly outlines as "the five levels of practical moral thinking."[5] For the religious giver of care the question is not so much "will I encounter human anguish and ecstasy?" but rather "how will I understand and respond to the sweep of human experience?" In broad form, this is the question of diagnosis and care. An adequate diagnosis is "transformational knowledge. . . .heavily influenced by wisdom emerging from praxis and is affected by the technical mandate to 'do something' to urgently alleviate. . ..suffering."[6] Adequate diagnosis assists us in evoking the terror and appreciating the beauty inherent in our life. Diagnosis can shape our response to tragedy and triumph.

As Western culture has grown in technical proficiency, the healing arts have experienced increasing pressure for diagnostic accuracy. The secular mental health world has responded to this pressure by developing a manual for diagnosis. The *Diagnostic and Statistical Manual*, Fourth Edition (DSM-IV) and its predecessors reflect this increased insistence for diagnostic accuracy These are valuable but incomplete documents. DSM-IV provides a standard diagnostic language for a breadth of professionals involved in the care of persons. However, all these manuals have been widely faulted for an inability to assess family dysfunctions or to assist the clinician in measuring the degree of legitimate guilt. In the opening example, one could assess the young man's Dysthymia and even note that he had Problems related to interaction with the legal system/crime. But one could not quantify his sense of despair or the longing of his father for the son's healing.

Within the religious community's counseling agencies it may still be the exceptional clinician who utilizes pastoral or religious criteria to diagnosis and guide his care of those seeking services. The author would note that this is a subjective impression, obtained informally through both collegial conversations and supervisory experience. The typical supervisory session appears to run something like this whenever the supervisor attempts to invite a religiously oriented diagnosis:

Clinician:	"So my diagnosis of this person is: Axis I Dysthymic Disorder, Chronic Axis II Deferred Axis III Chirrosis of Liver
Supervisor	"Could you tell me what your religious diagnosis is?
C:	"Well, she seems to have a lot of sadness.
S:	"Sadness is a religious theme?
C:	"Uh, no, uh, she seems to be alienated?
S:	"Are you telling me, or asking me?"

   Conversations among staff supervisors may be less tentative but no less impressionistic. Some persons may utilize Pruyser's schema of diagnosis. Many more are drawn to the use of Biblical stories or religious imagery to describe a person's dilemma. But even if there is general agreement around the core religious concerns, it is the author's experience that these conversations rapidly return to noting the psychological dynamics once the direction of treatment is discussed. Insurance claims could not be filed for client who presents with Profound Alienation or who describe their dilemma as a Crisis of Religious Faith. We will only note their depression or anxiety.
   The diagnostic system which follows provides caregivers with a schema around which they may organize the major religious or spiritual themes which bring people to them. While this system has implications for many of the pastoral functions such as preaching, education and church administration, the focus in this volume is on the task of delivering pastoral care or religiously informed counseling. Also, while the focus in this volume is primarily oriented toward describing problems, the author wishes to underscore that for a diagnosis to be complete there also needs to be an assessment of the positive values in a person's life. These positive areas hold much of the

strength with which the person addresses their basic quest to resolve their religious and spiritual dilemmas.

One final note on the purpose of diagnosis is in order. Providers of pastoral care and counseling work increasingly in an interdisciplinary setting. The contemporary local pastor will now have contact with several helping professionals who are involved in delivering care to persons also receiving pastoral care. These professionals come with the unified system of diagnosis inherent in DSM-IV. This is virtually the universal language of secular diagnosis. In order for religious clinicians to communicate effectively with the secular clinician, I have organized this religious system around a similar schema of axes. This structure may seem foreign to some pastors, for we are more at home with images of shamrocks, patterns in quilts, layers of meaning, slices of a pie and anecdotal stories to speak about the human condition. While these metaphors are rich in their evocative power, they cloud the task of collegial communication. Thus I have chosen to use three axes, rather than talk about three petals of a flower or three pieces of a puzzle to depict the way in which overlapping diagnostic concerns contribute to the whole identity which a person may bring to us for care and cure.

The Structure of Diagnosis

In a landmark work on the relationship between myth and the phenomenology of evil, Paul Ricoeur lays out a compelling schema. Our experience of evil moves from the most cosmic theme, *defilement,* through the religious realities, *sin,* to the most concrete of human activity, *guilt.*[7] Utilizing this outline in clinical practice, it appears that people are more motivated to seek care because of concrete ethical or behavioral considerations rather than by cosmic, philosophical or even religious matters. This does not imply that more universal themes are absent within the initial circumstances. But it does mean that persons who come for care want initial relief from suffering which is fairly concrete and may be hitting them in their pocketbook. The unresolved conflicts in religious values or a fundamental sense of existential dread may underlie their predicament. But the urgent mandate for healing most typically begins with *guilt.*

Thus the young man who is described at the beginning of the introduction needed foremost to receive assurances that he would not go to jail and would be able to continue planning for college. He needed to discover the limits of the punishment for his realistic guilt before we could discuss how defiled he felt by his own antecedent experience of molestation. His question which opened the doorway to explore his defilement was "where *was* God when those older boys were forcing *me* to expose myself?" did not surface in counseling for five months. This would become the life-long journey of his healing. The question came from the experience of his own initiation into the fellowship of the sexually molested. We needed to deal first with the ethical, legal and behavioral matters around confidentiality, cooperation with the courts and his adjustment to probation at home before any questions of meaning could be even asked. Only as his anxiety and hurt around these realistic matters were soothed could he begin to express his own feelings of sin and defilement.

As a result of such clinical experiences, realistic ethical concerns such as this are detailed on **Axis I.** Here the primary state is that of being punished, accompanied by a feeling of guilt. The task of healing for **Axis I** is that of seeking redress by both a cognitive assessment of ones' values as well as the emotional relief which accompanies solid empathic dialogue. The dominant diagnostic skills utilized to achieve these ends are empathy and inquiry. These skills may lead us in the direction of cognitive problem solving as well as affective relief of guilt and its attendant feeling of punishment. This axis invites the suffering person to engage in "a searching and fearless moral inventory."[8]

Religious caregivers frequently encounter persons whose ethical pain and affective guilt depict only the first layer of their distress. All too often the wounds which bring persons for care result from failures in relationships of trust. Whether the failure is the result of explicit betrayal or simply the inability of another to met one's need for care, the damage is much the same. The damage also appears to go deeper into the psyche and forms the basis of the repetitive search for an adequate or trustworthy other.

This phenomenon is so pervasive in the delivery of pastoral care that it merits separate attention. Thus on **Axis II** the caregiver can note the dimension of betrayal. Here the primary state is one of feeling violated and betrayed, either by another or by a god who has proven to be utterly inadequate. The primary feelings one encounters on this axis are terror and rage, which may be expressed either toward the self or toward the betraying other. The dominant diagnostic skills utilized along **Axis II** are those of consistency and self-awareness. Consistency in care provides the covenant into which a person may safely project the images of their failed gods one more time. Self-awareness in care is the capacity to examine our own adaptive responses to the person's expressed need. One cannot initially avoid such adaptive responses to another. The diagnostic moment comes when one articulates the explicit existence of such personal responses. The healing task on **Axis II** appears to be the grieving over the wounds of violation, the recognition that one has sinned, and a recovering an adequate sense of ultimacy. Here the religious caregiver is on familiar ground, for the traditional resources of religious communities have the cleansing of sin and the declaring of absolution as a primary institutional task.

In the life of the young man noted above, this level of healing discourse began as he spoke to his father about how desperately he had wanted the father to provide a protected space for *him* when he was a small child! Only as they wept together was their mutual grieving concluded. This laid the foundation for an articulation of more realistic and adequate expectations in their relationship.

There is yet a third layer of the soul whose pain we may have trouble acknowledging but whose anguish has sought the care of pastors for millennia. Those who stand at the door to this area may sit mutely in our office for moments or even hours. The descent through this door leads the person through our 20th century equivalent of The Tombs.[9] . These are persons whose inner experience is one of either being "in the wrong with Heaven."[10] or they sustain themselves with the awareness that they have received a unique revelation.

This primal experience of *defilement* is often experienced as profound abandonment by God, others, family and self. This state goes well beyond the simple belief that one has been misunderstood. Thus a third axis is utilized to note someone wrestling with such life-and-death spiritual themes. The primary feelings encountered on **Axis III** are mute anguish, disabling anxiety or pervasive depression. The distress at this level is chronic and extensive, with antecedents in catastrophic social stressors, genetic thought disorders and fundamental failures in parental care.

The diagnostic skills utilized for **Axis III** include an adequate familiarity with psychiatric diagnostic literature, clinical experience related to these disorders and appreciation for the way in which mythological themes may surface in the thoughts and relationships of persons. Less impaired individuals will reveal distress in **Axis III** through dream imagery, facial tics, awkward coughing, unexplainable tears or marked changes in appearance. Some religious caregivers may spend an entire career and encounter few individuals with distress at this level while others will seem to draw persons with this type of profound anguish. Thus one of the chief diagnostic skills is an awareness of the setting in which one serves as well as the typical persons who are likely to present themselves to you for care. A chief feature of distress at this level seems to be that of an experience of the Divine as being overwhelmingly close while also utterly unreachable.

The primary goal of healing on **Axis III** is a revisiting of the memory or event where the person sacrificed a portion of the self for a perceived greater good, whether of another or for the self. This is typically a lifelong journey in which it will be necessary to utilize the varied resources of traditional therapy, the sacraments, and potentially a vocational redecision. The fundamental goal of healing on this axis allows the person to take redemptive action which grows out of a healthy sublimation of what was once only silent chaos and anguished darkness.

The following text parallels the outline established thus far. In each part there is a chapter describing the diagnostic task. This is followed by a chapter outlining the specific affects associated with the distress and the diagnostic skills which help assess the person's condition. A third chapter then details the therapeutic movement toward health. Clinical vignettes which have been altered to assure confidentiality amplify the theoretical material in each chapter. I have chosen to use either single sex pronouns or third person plural pronouns rather than the awkward his/her, etc. in clinical examples to express my belief that care is not androgenous but is delivered either by individuals or a community. It is the author's hope that as caregivers read these chapters there will come a dawn of awareness about those for whom you care and about your own self.

Conclusion.
A final note to those who wonder about the efficacy of a unified

system of religious diagnosis and the use of the term "axis." When the intake interview on the young man noted above concluded, I wrote the following clinical diagnosis according to the rubrics of DSM-IV:

Axis I	Adjustment Disorder with Depressed Mood
Axis II	No Diagnosis
Axis III	No Medical Condition Reported
Axis IV	Problems related to interaction with the legal system / crime: accused of molestation of minor child
Axis V	Global Assessment of Function: Current: 65 Last Year: 85

The reader is invited to reflect on how your own understanding of this youngster's dilemma is shaped by your own diagnostic schema. The reader may also wish to ask, "how could I communicate this young man's spiritual distress to another caregiver?" It is to the ends of shaping our understanding, guiding our care of persons' wounds, and assisting us in collegial communication that this system of pastoral / religious diagnosis is offered. Using the outline suggested above his Religious Diagnosis would be stated as follows:

Axis I	*Ethical Guilt:* Molestation of a minor child
Axis II	*Covenantal Betrayal:* Recognition and resolution of his own molestation in early childhood
Axis III	*Existential Defilement:* Residual feelings of shame and stain from being molested and committing molestation

I realize that "axis" is a decidedly non-religious term. As noted above, however, the wider world of caregivers with whom we have to interface as providers of clinical and religious care all utilize a system of diagnosis which is organized around the metaphor of five axes. Communicating religious concerns to them is difficult enough without complicating the task with a diagnostic system organized around another rubric. The loss of religious imagery is made up for the facility with which this schema communicates religious concerns to social workers, licensed professional counselors, lawyers, psychiatrists and psychologists.

John Cox notes the following, "it can be argued that if mental health services in a multicultural society are to become more responsive to 'user' needs then eliciting this 'religious history' with any linked spiritual meanings should be a routine component of a psychiatric assessment, and of preparing a more culturally sensitive 'Care Plan.' "[11] This multi-axial system is offered as one way of gathering such a history, conducting such an assessment and developing such a care plan. The reader is invited to try this system of diagnosis within their caseload or pastoral visitation. Indeed one may wish to use this system alongside of another system, such as Pruyser's or Browning's. Evaluate this system within the real world of human care.

Part I:
Ethical Guilt and the Feeling of Blame

Chapter 1

Being Punished

"I waited until I fell in love and married the man of my dreams," she said with a wistful look. "One year later, he developed cancer." She paused. There was the hint of a tear behind the tight smile, "he died when our daughter was three years old. Why is God punishing me? I didn't deserve this!"

She feels depressed and overwhelmed with the task of being a single parent. She expresses loneliness. But these result from a primary loss. At the core of the loss is a feeling that she is being punished for an unnamed wrong. The details of her own childhood only amplified her feeling that this recent loss is but another verse in her litany of undeserved punishment.

Try as we might to tell ourselves we have done nothing wrong, the feeling of being punished persists whenever loss afflicts us or calamity strikes those we love. Coupled with the feeling of being punished is the inner scrambling to search for the blemish, sin or mistake that we can redress to avoid the continuing consequences of being punished. Such a frenzied scramble robs life of joy and creativity. If the losses occur at crucial developmental junctions, one's life can assume a quality of guarded anxiety or depression which cripples for decades.

Our language is full of metaphors that we "do not measure up," we "haven't made the cut," and that we have "missed the mark." Sometimes the mark we miss is tangible, like the "Stop" sign we run or the sales percentage we do not meet. Sometimes the measure we fall short of is an inherited standard about "the way our family ought to be" or "a Christian always begins the day with prayer." This is, indeed, our "first conceptualization of sin" which is "radically different from that of defilement" which is outlined "on the symbolic level." This particular way of symbolizing sin and fault "suggests the idea of a relation broken off."[12] Regardless of the standard's realism or origin, when we fail to meet the standard we feel guilty. We flinch. We brace ourselves for the punishment which our training has taught us to anticipate. Sometimes the anticipation is legitimate and the punishment which ultimately comes our way is real. At other times one is plagued by an anticipated punishment which never truly arrives except in the form of our own sleeplessness and worry.

One early religious story details the blessing and the curse at the core of human life.[13] Our first experiences with life tell us there are forbidden objects which produce direct and immediate consequences if we touch, spill or trespass upon them.[14] We fall away from the origin of our life. Our falling away produces in us the anticipation of punishment coupled with the feeling of shame.[15] This anticipation of punishment is more than a theoretical nicety. One need look no further than our sweaty palms whenever a police car follows us in traffic. Whether the moral law is written primarily upon our heart or remains externally focused, one does not help another's suffering by dismissing the anticipation of punishment as childish or irrational. The child we once were, and the creature of the universe we remain, does retain a fundamental awareness of vulnerability related to the things we may not touch or we shall surely die.

Ethical Realism in Diagnosis

"My lawyer said I'd better talk with you before filing our appeal," he said with an embarrassed smile. "The judge said I needed to spend some time in jail after hitting my girl friend. He didn't think I showed much remorse." There was a pause. "I'm sure sorry now," he added. "A year in jail will cost me my job and my reputation. I've got to find out what made me act so crazy."

Although there may be connections between one's background and current painful behavior, it is dishonest to equate empathy with justice. Adequate diagnosis must be ethically real. The emotional fact that this man suffered taunts from his mother and finally struck back at another woman's verbal taunts must not obscure the physical reality of the woman's broken rib. Part of his healing journey involved finally putting a realistic name on his mother's taunts. An equally important part involved his facing real legal guilt. Sometimes punishment is more than a feeling. There are situations when punishment is a legitimate component of the healing journey.

The estrangement of pastoral care from ethical thinking is well documented.[16] A clinician's lack of moral clarity or attempt to appear ethically neutral is particularly problematic in the task of diagnosis. Part of the pain which brings persons into counseling may be the long-standing failure to adequately name the wrongs done to them when they were vulnerable. A caregiver's reluctance to enter this ethical discussion creates two problems. Foremost it prevents the person from fully naming their pain. Second, it is re-traumatizing. Once again the individual must take care of someone else rather than attend to their own healing. Only this second time it is the therapist's ethical softness that the wounded person must soothe.

Caregivers have been hesitant to engage in ethical conversation due to an awareness that we are not judges, lawyers or juries. An undue emphasis on ethics can reduce the healing journey to an attempt to shape revenge or avoid relieving the relational pain resulting from current or past events. Thus it would be tempting with the gentleman noted above to spend the hour allowing him to recount his partner's questionable character, her attorney's courtroom taunting or his own musing about where she "really" got those bruises. Don Browning's work in the field of ethics and pastoral care outlines this pitfall very well.[17] Yet in the end we both had to recognize the reality of what a popular bumper sticker says, "You Can't Beat A Woman!"

Ethical realism in diagnosis means a willingness to assess the client's behavior, attitudes and life history within a recognizable and consistent framework of values. That a caregiver may immediately hear the internal supervisor query, "But *which* framework of values?" does not exempt us from this task. Unfortunately the religious caregiver often feels they must lay aside their very rich tradition of values in the interest of some ethereal standard of moral neutrality.[18]

The person in pain before us will not be helped by moral neutrality.
If anything, many persons bring the acute moral pain of discovering
that actions based on a supposed morally neutral world suddenly cause
very real guilt and the attendant feeling of being punished. Post-abor-
tion counseling is only one area where this dynamic is surfaced. Certainly the legal proceedings which may ultimately be initiated by a variety of hurting persons, or which may have begun to be brought
against them, rise from very real assumptions about the moral nature
of the human community.

A complete treatment of ethical theory is well beyond the scope of
this volume. However, the religious caregiver can be aided in the task
of diagnosis by acknowledging a single category of ethical reasoning:
prima facie guilt which results from the failure to execute one's *prima
facie* duty.[19] Coming from the ethical theory of W. D. Ross and others, this concept bids us realize that certain behaviors and attitudes
are, *on their face*, either morally binding or are, *on their face*, unethi-
cal and needing redress. Examples of a *prima facie* moral duty would
be the duty to do something because of my own previous actions. Such
a duty might include an act of reparation or an expression of gratitude
which would rest upon previous actions. Examples of a *prima facie*
moral wrong, according to Ross, might include a violation of the *duty
of non-maleficence,"* which would include child abuse in its many
forms, taking a human life, or violating another's trust."[20] In short,
the astute reader may recognize this list as the Ten Commandments.

Ethical realism also involves recognizing that the mere fact of some
personal difficulty does not explain away the emotional anticipation of
punishment or necessarily exempt one from real consequences of illegal action. Thus a parishioner who paid off one credit card by charg-
ing the debt to another credit card not only finally caved in with paralyzing fear but also had to contend with the very genuine demands of
creditors. No amount of psychotherapeutic talk about weak ego
boundaries or an addictive personality disorder would either satisfy her
creditors' rightful claims or ultimately soothe her inner moral pain.

Recognizing the Fear of Punishment

The most obvious indication of a person's fear of punishment is the
sentence which begins "I should have. . . .." and continues with a
statement outlining the standard that has been missed. Whether the
person could have reasonably met the standard or fulfilled the *prima*

facie duty is a matter to be considered as care unfolds. Initially it is important to hear the person's moral and emotional pain. "I should have covered the swimming pool," "I should have unplugged the coffee pot," I should have read the fine print," "I should have listened to her," are all statements that express the pith of pain and the limits of abilities.

Most frequently sadness, which may deepen into remorse or anxiety, festers into an inner posture of hypervigilence and accompanies the fear of punishment. These affects typically wind up with a clinical diagnosis of a *Condition Not Attributable to a Mental Disorder*, one of the Adjustment Disorders or the behavioral components of the more serious affective disorders such as Dysthymia, Bipolar Disorder and Anxiety Disorder. The personality disorders and the various addictions inevitably have ethically realistic components to the life-long pain associated with such grievous psychic wounds. While such ethical realism cannot be the terminus of care, neither can these ethical dimensions be overlooked. If one's addiction has roots in a parent's allowing him to drink at age five or because her parents still used marijuana recreationally well into her adolescence, a part of the urgent mandate of care does involve an adequate naming of these *prima facie* failures in parental nurture. These failures were ethically shattering to a vulnerable moral agent, i. e., a small child. It can be diagnostically helpful to note any conjunction between a person's punishment-directed affects and their recounting of major parental figures and settings. One can inquire about genuine events, with an eye toward relieving guilt, without necessarily casting oneself as a Grand Inquisitor.

Fear of punishment can also paralyze an otherwise competent person's ability to make a timely and effective decision. A recent loss, such as being fired from work, can make one hesitant to venture forth on a job search. Here the caregiver will need to gauge with the person the extent to which their discomfort is understandable tenderness vs. a revisiting of previous times when failure brought with it an experience of punishment. Such past experiences may find a voice in expressions such as "I just don't want to be hurt again," "I need some space," or "the last time I was in charge, somebody got killed." A diligent caregiver cannot initially assume that an individual's reluctance to come to closure with a situation is simply a matter of personal style.

"Remember how you felt in the fifth grade, when the big guys beat up on you and *nobody* would help you?" he said fiercely. "Well, I've been looking for work for 13 months. It feels like I've been in the school yard, alone, the whole time." His inward rage seemed to be almost choking him as he said, "I just want the punishment to stop."

"Being rejected for 13 months is brutal, punishing," I said. The opportunity to explore this poignant connection was at hand. But the doorway needed to be the realistic recognition of this man's experience. Even playground heroes have a limit to the punishment they can withstand. Crushing and repeated rejection had turned this once proudly competent person into someone haunted by an unseen but powerful punisher.

Fear of punishment can also lead someone to be overly decisive. In some particularly brutal households children and spouses can find themselves confronted by an enraged person whose hostility ceases only when an answer, *any* answer, has been provided to their interrogator. Since Western culture tends to value decisiveness, this fearful footprint's damage is more difficult to discern. Inviting out the memory which fuels the fear of punishment may take months of careful listening. Once again a part of the healing journey can be the mature reappraisal of the ethical setting in which the person made those first rapid decisions, as well as the lifesaving decision to "give the bastard *some* answer that will stop the punishment."

"Sinners in the hands of an angry god"

This is the basic description of the fear which we must touch if we are to deal religiously with the feelings of punishment. Even the most theologically sophisticated come to a point in life where they feel positively stalked by a Malevolent Force who has come for them. The Greek goddess of righteous anger, Nemesis, personifies this primal fear. It is a fear which seemingly drives narcissists the hardest. Well it might, for it was Nemesis who executed the binding punishment upon the original Narcissus.[21]

One need not know the content of such primal fear in another in order to hear and respect the fear. But one must be alert so as to respond to it when it is voiced. The core of such fear is not merely an emotion of vulnerability but, more commonly, such a feeling rests upon some violation of promise which the person has made to herself. If the caregiver can even tease out the shadow of this broken promise, one has come a great way toward soothing the fear of punishment which cripples many people.

The author remembers getting a telephone call from another Vietnam veteran. There had been an electrical fire in his home. His wonderful, life-filled daughter had been found cringing under her crib. She would live, but death would have been a mercy.

"I need someone to walk through the ashes with me," he said.

I went and we walked.

We walked in silence for several moments. They seemed to take us both back to another land and another time.

Finally he spoke. "This is the payback." It was all that he said. We embraced.

"Then it looks to me like the debt has been paid in full," I said through our tears. "May God's mercy come to you and to your daughter."

We need not look solely to the mythological traditions for this primal fear of punishment. It goes back to our own earliest heritage as Biblical people. Regardless of our views on the literary sources for many of the Scriptural writings, we must acknowledge the ethical reality of punishment meted out by a Just God. In our rush to deter the human action of revenge, we may overlook the moral force in the verse "vengeance is mine, saith the Lord."[22] There are times when it is basically more healing to acknowledge the legitimate dynamics of justice exacted upon a person than to seek always to explain away their fear of being punished.

There are a host of behaviors which carry very real but unfortunate consequences. There are attitudes which, when they become the basis of one's behavior, exert a damaging impact upon the lives of individuals and communities. As much as we might like reality to be different, it appears that there is something built into the nature of things such that a time of justice ultimately arrives. St. Paul calls this "the Wrath of God."[23] It is our basic recognition of this dynamic which drives us behaviorally and ethically, whether our recognition is informed by a religious or moral tradition or the simple brutality of hard life experience.[24]

Conclusion.

It is the author's clinical experience that some persons who seek care do so out of a desire to have their own re-emerging moral bearings confirmed. While this may be a far distance from the pastor proclaiming to the person "You are a sinner and need to repent," we may be able to use our considerable empathic skills to create a setting of safety in which the person may ultimately express this awareness herself. This heartfelt fear of punishment is most adequately addressed by the acknowledgment of guilt.

Chapter 2

Feeling Guilty

"Freddy did some *bad* things over there," he said of himself in the third person. His hands shook uncontrollably as he continued, "I just wanted to stay alive! Other people did *bad* things too." His face reddened and his eyes swept the room as though seeing his accusers arrayed against him. "Now I hear them calling me at night. 'We got your friends,' they say, 'We get you too!' "

Guilt is not equivalent with fault, especially moral fault.[25] Yet our practice as caring persons places us at the sword points of guilt and fault. The sting of guilt is one's inner presumption of fault, typically communicated through the dynamic of conscience. Again, while the full treatment of the ethical theory of conscience is beyond our present work, the caregiver may be assisted in the tasks of diagnosis and treatment by becoming familiar with the work of a single ethical theorist. Nicolai Hartmann argues persuasively that "values are not only independent of the things that are valuable, but are actually their prerequisite."[26]

This has immediate implications for the concrete tasks of diagnosis and treatment. First, the person's *feeling* of guilt is linked to a value which is ethically real and is antecedent to whatever behavior or attitude the person struggles with in counseling. Second, the ethical struggle itself is "a journey along the edge of an abyss."[27] The person

9

who seeks ethical direction in counseling may not be avoiding feelings and relationships. They may be telling the caregiver about a very genuine fight for their soul. Our modern age wishes to believe that human beings name values. But the wrecked hearts in our offices and sanctuaries remind us that what we value names us and maims us.

This is not new ethical ground for the religiously sensitive caregiver. Within one's religious tradition there is a recognizable moral code and attendant feelings of guilt whenever one violates the objective moral code. While the caregiver may wish to maintain a morally neutral attitude in the presence of a client's guilt, this may be an affective fiction on the part of the therapist. It may assist the therapeutic relationship if we do not leap out of our chair saying, "My God!!! You did *what!!??*" But it does not help the diagnostic task at all if we fail to distinguish ethically between the obsessive homemaker crushed by guilt over water stains on stemware and the schizoid mass murderer who feels no guilt after dismembering thirty-five people. Hartmann reminds us that "not all valuable things are of equal value. And the standard of moral goodness indicates exactly the boundary between worthy and unworthy intentions."[28]

The application of this principle to the task of diagnosis is this: we seek to discern the *client's* "boundary between worthy and unworthy intentions." At a later phase of care we may be invited to assist the other person as they evaluate the place of this boundary. We may even be invited to assist in the birth of a new boundary. However, the *initial* diagnostic task is to discover simply if, and how, the person's own value boundaries contribute to their current dilemma.

The connection between guilt and fault is made complex by the multiple sources which inform any of us about this boundary between worthy and unworthy intentions. Thus we may be in a setting with another person who has done nothing illegal or overtly immoral and yet who carries within a great feeling of pursuing unworthy ends.

The man had been unemployed for over a year. In desperation he found work as "a carpenter's helper. I guess that's all I'm really cut out to be," he would say with a sarcastic sneer. While he obviously valued work as a worthy intention, he just as clearly devalued not only his work mates but he felt guilty for having unworthy intentions. "Some of these guys are always going to be carpenter's helpers. But me, I know I'm going to be gone to the first desk job that comes along," he would say. "I feel crummy on this job. I'm pretending to be interested in this work and loyal to these people. I hate being this way." In addition to the way unemployment tore at his feelings of worthiness, being forced to work somewhere he would not freely choose to work created an ethical dilemma for this man. Whatever feelings of being a fraud might be fueled by personal narcissism, his recognition of disloyalty created a pain as real as his sore shoulder muscles after a 12 hour day.

Transcendent Values in Diagnosis

We must recognize in our diagnosis the legitimacy of realistic guilt which results from the violation of transcendent values. The basic outline of philosophic debate on transcendent values has not substantially changed since Kant's *Groundwork of the Metaphysic of Morals*. *If* we can know transcendent values, *how* we know them and *what we must do* in their presence is the gritty substance of ethical debate. Ethics still attempts to discern and promulgate the laws of free moral action.[29]

One addition to this complex discussion is the ethical theory of James Gustafson. He notes persuasively our life is in a world where values "are grounded in an objective reality of which human life is a part." What is so significant for our purposes here is Gustafson's recognition that our "experience of the ultimate power. . . .bearing down upon, sustaining and creating possibilities for action induces or evokes piety." This response of piety "requires that attention be given to deeply *affective* aspects of moral agents."[30]

The provider of care should not attempt to compile a definitive authorized list of transcendent values. Yet religious and secular communities typically do have such an authorized list. Modern liberal theology notwithstanding, there seems to be fairly common agreement among the various traditions about the values enshrined on such lists. Not many communities center themselves around values such as theft of property, taking another's life, speaking falsely or breaking promises. The diagnostic and treatment issues may be pointed around such ethical questions as "what do I do when two such values conflict?" as well as the primary ethical question of "what is the right and the good?" The employer who must fire a single mother for incompetence, knowing that her children will innocently suffer feels such pain. So too does the nurse whose oath binds her to care daily for the comatose patient whose family members never visit. For the care provider who is grounded within the Judaeo-Christian tradition, one central source of these transcendent values is the Ten Commandments. These are typically subdivided into commands which define one's relationship with the Holy and one's relationship with the neighbor (who is also holy). These values were aptly summarized by Jesus of Nazareth[31] and dynamically summarized by Immanual Kant, "act only on that maxim through which you can at the same time will that it should become a universal law."[32]

A person of the other major religions, Buddhism, Muslim and Hindu share in this inner experience of being "born down upon" by similarly compelling transcendent values.[33] Such values may be encountered in the arena of family life, culture, religious dogma or the privacy of the heart. But rest assured, they shall make themselves known to each of us. It can be helpful to both diagnosis and treatment for the caregiver to become conversant with these other traditions.

It is unhelpful and dishonest for the clinician to either mix all such values into an eclectic ethical soup or to deny *a priori* a transcendent legitimacy of any value. Indeed such a carefully crafted posture of ethical "neutrality" in a pastoral setting may impede the formation of the very therapeutic alliance which we know to promote healing empathy. The person with religious sentiment may be dismayed at a caregiver's perceived distance from the values of her tradition while the secular person may be confused by a religious caregiver whose moral affect is masked.

The person noted above who was out of work for 13 months commented in a subsequent conversation, "I found out that my last employer had canceled my health insurance six months before whimsically firing me. He said it was a 'cost cutting move.' I didn't find out about it until I took my wife to the hospital to have our child!" Clearly there was a violation of law here, not the least of which was the breach of an employment contract. In reflecting upon the company's action and the employee's anguish a judge's final comment here was that the company's action violated "fundamental human decency." While one may have trouble identifying the precise transcendent value involved here, few fail to recognized that a greater value bears down on both employer and employee here besides the legitimate pursuit of corporate profits. As Stackhouse notes, "there is a universal moral order, rooted in the righteousness of God, which is other than ordinary experience yet directly pertinent to ordinary experience."[34] The religiously sensitive counselor brings the awareness of such a moral order into the counseling relationship by virtue of their being and perhaps their training. Those whose ethical pain compels them to seek care do so within a moral framework. An important part of both diagnosis and care is to allow the individual an opportunity to articulate their moral framework, re-evaluate their framework if necessary, and continue their life's direction. Such an enterprise will involve all aspects of the person's life, including personal cognition, emotions and piety. This process will also envelope their wider family and societal relationships. Such a re-evaluation will necessarily move beyond the consideration of ethics and guilt, but these can be places to begin the inquiry.

Recognizing the Transcendent Value

She clearly did not want to be in the counselor's office. Her physical shaking and quavering voice were amplified by the statement, "I *never* thought I would come to someone for help! But here I am! And there's not easy way to say this. My boy friend has AIDS! I love him! My religious values remind me that Jesus loved lepers and ate with outcasts. But I cannot!! I feel angry! Angry with God! Angry with *him* for doing such a *stupid* thing! Angry with myself for being unable to do what I know I ought to do."

Few people come to a place of caring able to identify the transcendent value upon which they are caught. But many come with a recognition that they are unable or unwilling to do what their moral and religious instincts tell them they *ought* to do. Transcendent values exert categorical force. Anger, resentment, depression and anxiety typically alert us to the presence of some strong conflict within the person. But these affective indices are too general by themselves to assist one in identifying the specific content of an ethical conflict. Often we see the affect produced by such a categorical force long before we identify the value at the origin of the affect. Thus our *prima facie* affective clinical experience may not be a completely adequate guide to discern the transcendent values at the root of the person's anguish.

Persons who come for care may be in one of several moral situations. They may be in direct conflict with one or more explicit moral values. A client who supported his $500 a day heroin habit by shoplifting said, simply, "I should not have stolen the merchandise. I was drugged out crazy at the time I stole the stuff. But all the same, I should have gone for help rather than steal."

They may also be at the junction of several equally good moral values. The familiar example known to every first year philosophy student: "do I tell the ax-wielding madwoman at my doorway that her husband is in my basement? Do I tell the truth and become an accessory to homicide or do I lie in order to preserve life?"

The religiously oriented caregiver has several moral grids through which to view another's estrangement with transcendent values. The five levels of practical moral thinking outlined by Browning is an excellent guide to ethical diagnosis within a clinical setting.[35] James Gustafson's four-point pattern of discernment provides a similar matrix by which a caregiver may assist someone in organizing both the content and affects of the value which bears down upon them.[36] . Likewise one may use any number of "authorized lists" of transcendent values to help the client state their moral dilemma. The Ten Commandments,[37] the Beatitudes,[38] St. Paul's treatise on love,[39] or one of his many lists of common virtues[40] would be well known to many religious persons. The Boy Scout Law contains an admirable list of positive transcendent values.[41]

The diagnostic task is to allow the person opportunity to identify their current dilemma in explicitly moral terms, if such are appropriate. The clinician errs in directing a person away from moral inquiry just as much as when they fail to attend to a strongly expressed affect. The young woman cited above felt caught by several transcendent moral demands: be perfect, be loyal, be unconditionally loving. These were painfully focused within the mores of her highly religious family. This relational component of her pain also needed to be addressed during our work, for she worshipped her parents. At its root, ethical guilt contains the conflict between our own status as a moral agent and our longing at times for there to be another, any other, onto whom we may shift some of our responsibility.

Soothing the Anguish of Guilt

The jagged edges of guilt may be soothed but the scars on the heart and within our history remain. Sometimes the soothing can be achieved through a cognitive reassessment of my past or present situation. Often guilt may be soothed by the emotional relief which comes from unburdening the self within a caring relationship. Acting to transform my situation or to act upon new moral values when facing a formerly paralyzing decision can also relieve the burdens of a guilty heart. But nowhere is that a sterile ethical field, where a single decision rights all previous wrongs or a flash of insight insulates us from all future trials.

Although a person's cognitive reassessment of their moral code makes for somewhat dull reading, the success of such a treatment strategy with depression and anxiety is well known.[42] There are always feelings that need to be resolved from past wounds. But there comes a time when one may need to simply acknowledge "I was 5 and could not have known more information or acted any differently than I did." This is a step in one's moral development not unlike a religious conversion. But just as we do not require every convert to be knocked off a horse by a blinding light,[43] neither should we assume that every therapeutic resolution necessitates a great quantity of affective pyrotechniques.

"I didn't like the way you did it, at first. But now I see that I've been helped," she confided at our termination session. "I wanted a single answer that would tell me how I could love my boyfriend, forget about his AIDS and hide it all from my parents. You supported me while I thrashed around in this confusion, but you didn't give me the answer."

Support from a caregiver, especially during the initial anguish of one's effort at gaining relief, can help lift the weight of guilt. Our empathic stance communicates to the person "I am here with you. Your pain and confusion does not frighten or offend me." Such empathy is crucial if the other person is to ever reassess their moral values. Only from a stance beside another can we begin to see their world, understand the forces which bore down upon them so heavily that no other choice seemed possible, and help them find their own voice instead of the mute suffering of guilt.[44]

Our guilt is soothed most completely when we join a new community of moral formation and discourse. Whether one joins a non-abusive family through marriage, a caring cadre of companion sufferers such as Narcotics Anonymous, or a vital and receptive religious congregation, such a transition feels like nothing short of a rebirth. It is within such a community that one is not only "born down upon" by a new set of transcendent values but, more significantly, one finds new values and companions who lift them up.

Conclusion

Throughout this entire process the religious caregiver will be confronting their own values.   What can be most helpful to both diagnosis and treatment is our own concordant wrestling with angels - - those moments when we hear and see our own moral limits within the story of the wounded other.   In such times both client and caregiver rediscover the dynamics of mercy and grace.   It is also in such moments that the wounded one may begin to see a way of truly redressing the feelings of blame, punishment and guilt.   It is to this subject that we now turn our attention.

Chapter 3

Seeking Redress

The mailing looked like it came from a community service group. But I saw that the return address was that of a prominent attorney. "I wonder what she's up to now," I mused while opening the envelope. Inside was a brochure informing the reader of a recent change in Virginia's legal code. Although the law was overturned on an appeal, it was possible for awhile for persons victimized by incest to press criminal and civil charges upwards of two years after the person had received communication from a physician, psychiatrist or clinical psychologist "that the cause of his/her depression, eating disorders, etc., is the result of childhood sexual abuse." The brochure continued, "regardless of when communication occurs, after June 30, 1992 all suits must be filed by age 28." The brochure concluded "regardless of what the final decision may be about whether or not to file suit, it is essential that all adult survivors of childhood sexual abuse be informed of their rights under the new law as soon as possible."

Historically the Church and religious caregivers have resisted contact with the courts. Some professional providers of pastoral care and legal counsel asks clients to sign a document which state, in part, "I understand that the counselor is not required to testify in a court proceeding, and I further agree that I shall not request my counselor to testify." This is a position which comes out of both Scripture[45] and the sacrament of confession and absolution.

Nevertheless, contemporary religious caregivers face a multifaceted dilemma. First, some clients come to counseling with an awareness that they desire some type of redress. This delves right to the heart of our personal and institutional life. Additionally, such intake documents offer no protection in the face of laws which require the positive reporting of the physical and sexual abuse of minors. Second, feminist research on counseling in matters related to sexual molestation and rape suggest the therapeutic value of victims actively pursuing those who perpetrated the injury through either the civil or criminal court. Third, although we make much in theory about the sanctity of the confessional, it is quite another matter to have someone who, after some conversation in our office says, "I must tell you now about the body I buried fifteen years ago. . . .." or "we have been distributing cocaine for years. I want to stop, but if I leave the organization, I'm sure I'll be killed. Can you help me?"

Such confessions make good novels. For some care providers, these words are more than a writer's fiction. When these words are spoken in your office, one quickly realizes that there can be more to counseling than the affective relief of suffering. We may not have heretofore construed our role as one that offers more than such relief. Until such words are spoken! Regardless of how we initially define our role, once such words *are* spoken in our presence, the matters of diagnosis and treatment take on an additional degree of seriousness. The matters of "how do we name this pain?" and "how might this pain be relieved?" now involve the caregiver and seeker in a journey which includes the broken soul of society. We may be compelled to enter the arena in which this brokenness awaits like a roaring lion to consume all who enter.

Naturally the matters of redress also relate to a person's responding in a new way toward those they have wounded. Healing can bring one to a new level of awareness of their own capacity to change their life's direction. A part of the healing journey may include acts of restitution or words of apology to those one has wronged. This step brings an added layer of relief from the feeling of punishment. It also shifts the identities and balance of power within the immediate social network of the person who comes for care.

The author remembers dozens of veterans from several wars for whom a significant part of their healing involved a return to the land of battle. Not all battles are fought in distant lands. Not all warriors have the courage to return to the original site of brutality and wounding. But for those who do, and for those who accompany them, such journeys are among the deepest soothings one can witness. This chapter explores the alternative avenues of redress, regardless of the place of the battle or the status of the combatants.

When One Has Been Wronged

"The abuse started when I was two, I think. Certainly by the time I was three, my older cousins had already had fights over who got 'first dibs' on me," Paul continued quietly. "I can sort of understand their actions, because they're what we called 'half-wits.' But who can give back to me the trust that my uncles and my aunt took away from me? I am terrified of getting close to men and not too fond of women, although they're a bit easier."

Paul took a deep breath. Then came a cry from his depths, "they stole my childhood and God *damn* them! They ought to *pay!*"

We would journey together through these painful swamps of his torn childhood. No matter how far he roamed into the depths, he returned to this theme: somehow there should be justice, if not for him then justice upon those who had inflicted such continuing horror upon his soul. He felt torn between the desire for these wrongs to be made right and his religious training which apparently compelled him to forgive the ones who were unaware of the depth of damage their humiliation had wrought upon him.

Persons seek to redress their wounds out of a desire to move beyond their roles as victims. Seldom is their motive entirely pure. Seldom does one obtain a complete cure for the damages endured in life. Even though justice and healing may be incomplete, which of us would choose the running sores of continued victimization over the tangible relief which might be gained through redress? Indeed some argue that the transcendence of suffering includes active behavior which helps reshape the person's situation.[46]

As indicated earlier, for many persons it is redress enough to simply acknowledge that they were wronged. For others, there can be a widening circle of persons to whom they acknowledge their woundedness and current degree of healing. From the privacy of a therapeutic relationship to public disclosure to transformation toward a new vocation, many find satisfying avenues to reshape the gashes in soul, psyche and soma.

Thus Paul came for support during his last year in medical school. He struggled with these obvious wounds from childhood which tore at his very soul. As he returned to the anguish of the wounds, he wondered aloud "what must I do now, with the children who remain near to these people?" Not an idle question for either this soon-to-be pediatrician or the now-grown adult who could just as easily be driving a truck. The ethical and behavioral dimensions of redress would remain the same: what is his current responsibility toward those who might yet be victimized? This too is part of the urgent mandate which brings wounded people to the place of healing.

It does help to examine real alternatives, come to some practical decisions about future action and then implement the plan while in a supportive or therapeutic relationship. This had two benefits for Paul. First, it legitimated his concerns in a way that affective symptom relief would not. His feelings were tied to historical events and the current actions of real people. He did not wake up one fine morning deciding to be depressed and full of rage. Second, as care progressed he became able to negotiate his way through the complex web of decisions related to these continuing social and family relationships. He no longer needed to accept uncritically the victimizing demands of his family or the terrorizing rage of his still-wounded memory.

But there are times when the only way of redressing a wound is the court system. We may be requested to provide care for any number of persons who have been wronged by a person or an institution. Whether the request comes from the person wronged or through an attorney, the underlying matters of care remain essentially the same: how can we assist this person in naming his pain within this new arena and how does this context of pain guide our care?

For Rosalie, a tender second grader, the fondling by a grandfather previously convicted on charges of child molestation brought feelings of sadness, poor grades and rebellious conduct at home. She and her mother first sought redress through counseling and a family intervention. This intervention was guided by a local private therapist. It was agreed during this session that "Pa-Paw" would pay for Rosalie's counseling. He also agreed to re-enter group counseling.

But when the first bill arrived from Rosalie's therapist, Pa-Paw reneged on his agreement. After some added consultation with Rosalie's therapist, the mother decided to seek redress through the courts. She filed a complaint with the county's department of social service. After a brief investigation, the department and Rosalie's mother sought redress through the courts. At a formal hearing, the charges of molestation were certified and Pa-Paw's probation was revoked. He was remanded to counseling and to pay up to $1,000 for Rosalie's counseling.

Did action through the court help Rosalie and Pa-Paw? The resolution seemed to relieve Rosalie's depression. She seemed to regain her playfulness. She commented that although "it was scary" seeing the judge, it was no more scary than being fondled by her grandfather. Primarily she felt believed by someone powerful. Adults she did not previously know (judge, therapist, social worker) took her seriously and trusted her word. This posture took her out of the role of victim and restored her to the role of citizen. She learned that she could take initiative and respond to a serious problem. Obtaining redress through the court system provided a significant if not complete response to the developmental wounds produced by her molestation.

The provider of religious counseling as well as the secular clinician may have theoretical difficulties with such a case. If so, referral is the ethical course of action. We have no right to attempt to talk someone else out of their legal right of redress simply because we believe that healing may lie in another direction. There is one additional matter which the provider of care must face: when is the perpetrator finally held responsible for their wounding behavior? Is it always someone *else's* failure of attitude, incomplete parenting, underpaying job, etc. to which we redirect our attention? Such social questions impinge on the initial decision whether or not to offer care to one who may become involved in legal action.

When One Has Been an Agent of Wrong

But what of Rosalie's Pa-Paw? How might he redress the pain inflicted by his own hand? Clearly it was his inability or unwillingness to do so, or to face his guilt, that resulted in an extreme measure being taken. Unless the provider of care, whether pastoral or secular, works within a prison setting, few clinicians will have significant or sustained contact with persons who have been brought to this level of redressing their wrongs.

More typically, the clinician will encounter people who come to some level of self-awareness that they have caused another person significant, life-altering pain. At such a point the person may cry out "what must I do? . . ..what *can* I do?" Such moments are poignant to be sure. This is also a moment in which a caregiver can adopt a posture of walking with the person through concrete options for behavioral change.

The levels of redress when one has been an agent of pain parallel the avenues of healing for the victim. For some, the most that can be hoped is that they obtain some private level of soothing for their own hearts and minds. Supportive and insight-oriented therapy as well as the traditional rites of the faith community such as confession and penance can help. For others, there are avenues of genuine contact with those who have felt the impact of their prior behavior. Such contact can be guided during a therapeutic process or through one of the Anonymous programs. The Eighth and Ninth Steps of Alcoholics Anonymous can be effective guides in such a journey: "Made a list of all persons we had harmed, and became willing to make amends to them all; Made direct amends to such people wherever possible, except where to do so would injure them or others." To begin to *wonder* about such steps is healing. To *walk* with another who decides to take the steps is indeed a holy quest for client and clinician.[47]

Assessing the avenues for redress open to one who has been the perpetrator, the clinician may once again choose to walk with the person through cognitive moral inquiry. To help the person articulate the promise that was broken, the boundary which was crossed, the perceptions which were so skewed that they led to unfortunate actions can be healing. Clinicians using either cognitive or affectively oriented therapeutic techniques achieve beneficial results.

As the landmark work of James Fowler illustrates, the step from one level of moral awareness to the next is an arduous one.[48] Yet walking with someone through this conversion is a legitimate role for pastoral and secular care. The person who is thus transformed is a new creation.[49] From such a new standpoint, the person can now approach the task of more direct redress with resources of spirit heretofore unavailable to them.

This may appear to be a simple process for a clinician. Unfortunately, without careful thought such action can degenerate into unbridled manipulation of all parties by an underlying desire for clarity and closure. The ones providing care in such situations often find their own values challenged. Healing for perpetrators and victims in the realm of ethics is a process of dialog in which we are invited to stand with one and sometimes both sides of a tortured, tangled relationship. As much as we would like there to be a sterile ethical field upon which to stand, there appears to be only the mud of a crowded No Man's Land. We long for a guide to make completely clear lines of responsibility, guilt, innocence and forgiveness. Such is not possible. We have left both the Garden and Mt. Sinai long ago.

It seems to the author that here the pastor has one distinct advantage. We are outside the rubrics of legal evidence. We deal primarily in the wounded perceptions of persons. Thus our dialog with hurting persons, regardless of their role in the suffering, most often focuses more on restoring the relationship rather than assigning blame. Making this point as clearly as possible, even in the realm of ethics, can free all parties to truly re-examine their values at some future point. This is a particularly powerful process to undertake once the feelings of punishment have been redressed and whatever balance possible has been restored to the relationship.

Conclusion

In summary one should note that this first **Axis** attempts to make explicit the ethical boundaries within a person's dilemma. Here the clinician should seek to describe and depict the ways in which those boundaries have been transgressed, either by the person or a significant other person. While it has not been illustrated in these chapters, the clinician may also wish to state on this **Axis** the positive moral resources available to both client and clinician. These too influence healing in a major but not always obvious manner.

Part II:
Idolatry and the Feeling of Betrayal

Chapter 4

Being Violated

_____

He is a large man. When he stands close to you there is an immediate sense of physical power. Seventy-seven years line his face. His eyes still carry the fire which was placed there as a young man.

"I was one of the suiciders," he said. "They told us we could handle seven men, with a knife or our hands."

There was a pause. I had the feeling that the after dinner conversation had taken a decidedly serious turn.

"I've talked to pastors and counselors before, but no one has been able to tell me 'why I am *still* this way?" he persisted. *This way* meant his awareness that he could still find that place of grim power within his heart and act violently without a moment's warning. "I wasn't *this way* before the training," he concluded. "I was glad to serve, but I have never been the same."

It didn't take a combat veteran to hear this man's core of despair. For just a moment his eyes hinted at the softness of his seventeenth summer.

Two weeks later, another man spoke of his six years military service as a pilot in the China-Burma-India Theater. He flew "The Hump" into China, dodging Japanese long-range fighters amid the perils of uncharted mountain passes. His eyes also clouded as he recalled those days.

"They took me right out of college, put me in an airplane and made me a pilot! I loved it! Gosh!! It's making my hair stand on end just to remember those times!" he exclaimed.

Two human beings had been fundamentally changed by their exposure to something larger than their self and their world. For one, the life-changing impact propelled him in a hopeful and productive arc back into the community. For the other the change imploded into a marginal life. Both continue to live out the implications of this change, inside and outside of the church, despite their advancing age. Ultimately the Suicider took his own life while the Humpmaster was elected to the board of yet another community agency.

When the core of our personality is transformed by contact with something greater than our Self, we are violated. If the transformation is positive, we use the language of salvation and hope to speak about the experience. If the transformation carries us into a negative orbit, then we use metaphors of damnation and despair. But the core data of the experience is one of transcendent violation.

We are shaped by forces that overwhelm our conscious choices. These forces influence us in ways which are subtle, like the disapproving clucking of a mother's tongue or the fleeting scent of sandalwood in a Buddhist temple. They may also forcibly take us where we would never choose to go, whether in the flash flood that roars thorough a valley at 2:35 a.m. or the predatory father who insists his daughter take care of him. Such forces may also be cultural and come with all the reinforcements of social acceptance or banishment. The beautifully thin, blonde teenage girl, the black clad member of the SWAT Team and the Preacher Boy who harangues an audience for 2 hours without a breath each give us a living picture of an invisible god. But what sacrifice do such gods demand? What does one do when such gods fail? How does one leave such divinities and forge a new life?

These questions and their adjunct concerns are the focus of this second **Axis**. Our varied religious heritages offer a singular caveat: we *may* succeed in naming the idol but we will not succeed in eradicating the god whom it represents.

Naming the Idol in Diagnosis

The pile on the table is always quite impressive. Keys to a Mercedes Benz may lie beside an archer's shooting glove. A Scofield Reference Bible might repose beside a pitch pipe. Sometimes a bottle of Jack Daniel's or a pack of Marlboro's join the montage. "I want you to bring an idol to next week's class," I've instructed them. For those who need a bit more direction, I will add, "make it something you center your life around. Something you might kill or die for. Bring something that has made you the person you are or hope to become."

In the religious literalism of our youth, we may have assumed that because we were not offering our first-born child to Molech we were not worshipping any idols. But a pastor can identify any number of objects and goals to which persons offer themselves, their resources, children and futures. In the broadest religious terms, the diagnostic question is simply "what is the name of your idol?" and not "is there an idol which you worship?" Our violating idols are primarily something, or someone, whose legitimate worth or power has become overly valued. Some idols have explicitly religious names and recognized ceremonies. But the more insidious ones which drive hurting persons to our doorstep are the implicit principalities, thrones and powers we are absolutely convinced we cannot live without.

The unfolding tragedy of Jonestown spread across the newspaper's front page in what is typically called Second Coming type. "How awful and incomprehensible," exclaimed a woman in my parish. She spoke for all of us. Here was a situation of clear and explicit idolatry which finally took the lives of over 900 adherents. Learning the details about the tragedy, and the decade of events which preceded it, one could discern the familiar patterns of religious recruitment, individual conversion and gradually increasing isolation of the cult from the mainstream.

Jonestown is not even the most recent incarnation of a more fundamental process of life-transforming religious violation. What is the difference between the uniform of tennis shoes, black pants and button-down white shirts of the Heaven's Gate cult and the plain clothes worn by a member of Old Order Baptist group who sat in my parish office struggling over continued membership in the "church?" She said, "I have decided to leave my husband and the Church. In our community this will mean that I will no longer exist." So often one community's faithful presentation of God can be wounding and even homicidal to some of its own members.

Naming the idol in diagnosis can be a difficult and delicate task. Yet as one practitioner aptly notes, "the task of taking on the gods is at the heart and soul of pastoral counseling."[50] We can suggest three broad categories in which one may search for idols: explicit religion, implicit religion and secular religion. Each area has some recognizable gods. Their violation of our selves and their sacrificial demands gravely affect our well being. They may even inhabit - and inhibit - our consulting room and our pulpit. The presence of religious belief in human beings, whether explicit or implicit, is pervasive and the clinician ignores this data at peril to both self and client.[51]

Visible Gods of Explicit Religion

The area of explicit religion contains gods who are supported by a belief system which the worshipper can elucidate. Explicit idols are a perversion of genuine religious faith. They typically use portions of one or more faith groups, creeds and rites to undergird their belief and piety. An explicit idol can influence religious traditions which are polar opposites, primarily because they appeal to our more fundamental broken, prideful nature. An implicit idol can be a deeply rooted personal habit or group practice which overwhelms the self. Addictions and the various sexual perversions take up residence here. Secular idols reveal themselves through the overwhelming press of cultural values. The various "isms" and fads of our age live here. The most notorious ones are those we cannot see except in the shadows of our perceived personal and national enemies.

The god of Fundamentalism makes an appearance in every age and in every faith group. Regardless of the cause for which one enters this god's service, its chief signature is the *demand that there is only one right way or viewpoint* on any matter. This god appeals to our primary desire for an unchanging center within a dynamic world. We long for a singular lens through which all reality will assume an unmistakable clarity. This god supplies such clarity as well as the motivations for extreme self-sacrifice. It is also the one in whose name we slay or excommunicate our perceived enemies. In religious areas this god has an appeal which spans the theological spectrum. The inerrancy-testing conservative is no more vulnerable to this god's sway than the coercive, politically correct liberal or the hallelujah shouting Pentecostal.[52]

The litmus test of this god comes at the crossroads where one must choose to hold on to the world as interpreted by this god or accepting a new interpretation as witnessed to by one's neighbor. This deity's appeal is particularly seductive to established religions. Fundamentalism frequently surfaces as a response when too much social or theological change has occurred too rapidly.

The god of Cargo is another well-known religious deity. While it was first noted by anthropologists researching Pacific Island cultures, its appeals are to a broader province. This god's primary attraction is liberation. The chief domain of the Cargo god is in the religions of the oppressed. In this god's world, something awful is currently happening to the worshipper. All this awful stuff will stop *and a savior will arrive with cargo,* if the worshipper makes the requisite changes. If the cargo does not appear, it is because the worshipper has not tried hard enough or carried out the prescribed ritual in the precise fashion.

The power of this god comes from realistic suffering. This suffering can be genuine physical deprivation and poverty. This suffering may also be fueled by economic envy, emotional abuse or co-dependency. To suggest that waiting for the cargo is a bogus hope or that the tragedy is the normal suffering of life is to court the charge of heresy from the god's adherents. One may chuckle privately at another's obsessive rituals, such as checking fifteen times to turn off the stove or saving every scrap of newspaper because it might be needed someday. But the security and salving of cargo, and the need for ritualistic precision, becomes understandable when facing the terror of losing a home or enduring the hunger of the Great Depression.

A final major religious idol has become popular in the 1990's. This is the god of Trendy Disbelief. This deity cloaks spiritual poverty in brilliant robes and requires a sacrifice of theological integrity. Where other gods may reveal themselves in an attitude of zeal, this god's signature is that of studied inattention to religious affect. Persons who worship this god appear to have an urbane shell surrounding them about formal religion. They may also express a general religious sentiment about "belief in a God." But when pressed, the content level of their disbelief may be on the par with third grade Sunday school material.

Some Trendy Disbelievers are more concerned to appear cosmopolitan than specifically religious, so they cloak the neglect of their children's religious education in the robe of intellectual freedom. "I'm letting the children decide for themselves about their religious belief," they may say. Others weave together a shiny garment made out of swatches from several theologies - a bit of New Age dazzle, some Buddhist compassion and maybe a spicy Jewish wisdom story. This garment and god serve them well until major tragedy strikes. Then they discover they have no consistent core of religious value to anchor them in the storm. They are suddenly challenged to abandon current fashion for a living encounter with a viable tradition of faith - and the God Who Lives. It is hard for such worshippers to admit that they need the very Deity they formerly decreed was not very important. It is usually easier for them to complain about being suddenly alone. They do not seem to realize that the Deity has answered their prayer and treated them as the adult they portray themself to be - the Deity has left them to feel the full impact of their freely chosen religious values.

A final note before leaving the area of religious idols. Secular counselors have a particularly difficult time judging healthy from unhealthy religious faith. Unfortunately this often prompts them to develop a stance which may see all religions as problematic or all religious matters as outside of their perview.[53] Secular counselors may also be prone to committing the syncretic error. This error takes form whenever we blur the very real distinctions between various religious rites and values. Dr. Howard Clinebell's describes the direction of healthy religion in a helpful series of statements, some of which are listed below. I commend these to you as a way of gauging the relative health of any god - whether Trendy, Cargo or Fundamentalist.[54] Clinebell's comments may be particularly helpful for assessment in an age when many persons lack connection with a coherent religious tradition.

Do the Religious Beliefs, Attitudes and Practices
of persons

- give them a meaningful philosophy of life that provides trust and hope in facing the inevitable tragedies of life?

-    provide creative values and ethical
  sensitivities that serve as inner
  guidelines for behavior that is both
  personally and socially responsible?
-    provide an integrating, energizing, growing
  relationship with that loving Spirit that
  religions call God?
-    inspire an ecological love of nature and a
  reverence for all life?
-    provide for a regular renewal of basic trust
  by affirming a deep sense of belonging
  to the universe?
-    bring the inner enrichment and growth that
  comes from 'peak experiences?
-    offer the person a growth-enabling community
  of caring and meaning?
-    build bridges rather than barriers between
  them and persons with differing values
  and faith systems?
-    enhance love and self-acceptance (rather
  than fear and guilt) in their inner life?
-    foster self-esteem and the 'owning' and using
  of their strengths in constructive living?
-    stimulate the growth of their inner freedom
  and autonomy?
-    help them develop depth relationships
  committed to mutual growth?
-    encourage the vital energies of sex and
  assertiveness to be used in affirmative,
  responsible ways rather than in repressive
  or people-damaging ways?
-    foster realistic hope by encouraging the
  acceptance rather than the denial of reality?
-    provide them with effective means of moving
  from the alienation of appropriate guilt
  to healing reconciliation with themselves,
  others and God?

- encourage creative development in their
  beliefs and values through the life cycle to
  keep these congruent with their intellectual
  growth?
- provide effective means of keeping in touch
  with the creative resources of the unconscious through living symbols, meaningful
  rituals and vital myths?
- encourage them to keep in touch with both
  the soft, nurturing, receptive, feeling side
  and the assertive, rational, intentional,
  ethically demanding side of their personalities
  and their religion?
- make them aware of person-hurting
  institutional practices and motivate them to
  work to change these forces that oppress
  potentializing on a massive scale?

.

Invisible Powers of Implicit Religion

Now let us turn to some idols of implicit religion. They too carry
their own structure of belief and piety. They sometimes have their own
holy writings, sacred places of gathering and rites of initiation. Their
only distinction may be that they are not explicitly tax exempt and that
some of their rites may be illegal.

Dionysus, the god of pleasure, has taken on the formidable persona
of addictions in our time.[55] Addictions wield significant influence in
our culture. Who has looked into the eyes of a baby going through
crack withdrawal or listened to the grieving of a mid-life alcoholic and
not seen Dionysus' violation? Dionysus offers us salvation by promising to transform our life. This deity has power to violate us from the
very moment of our conception, as evidenced by Fetal Alcohol Syn-
drome. The rites and beliefs of Dionysus infect our family structures
and language for generations. Dionysus teaches us the dynamics of
denial and rewards deception. The social cost of Dionysian rites can
devastate entire neighborhoods more extensively than a Category 4

hurricane. Insofar as the various substances do, indeed, alter our fu--ture from what and who we might otherwise have become, Dionysus can be said to deliver what his religion promises.

The various Anonymous programs take the religious component of addiction very seriously. They recognize that the addict is facing a crisis in religious belief and not simply a pharmacological problem. Given the pervasiveness of the world's drug supplies, devotees and refugees of Dionysus will be in every worship service, mosque, ashram and consulting room until the end of time. In this sense the worship of Dionysus is eternal. Paradoxically although many worship Dionysus in some form, few readily name him. Dionysian faith may be the best illustration of the ancient belief that to name a god is to finally have power over the god.

The essentially spiritual dilemma at the core of addictions of all types is made eloquently by Peter Tractenberg in his study of sexual addiction:

> "at the center of every addiction, as at the center of every cyclone, is a vacuum, a still point of emptiness that generates circles of frantic movement at its periphery. . . It is character-ized not only by a feeling of worthlessness, the conviction that one deserves nothing more than the destiny of a drunk or a junkie, but by a blurred and tenuous sense of self--a fundamen-tal uncertainty about one's own existence."[56]

Venus, goddess of love and beauty, is surrounded by mystery and rites of initiation. Like all deities she has the power to bless and curse those devoted to her. Venus is fueled by the fundamental capacity to create life. With the emergence of the HIV virus and other genetically transmitted diseases, the creative sexual act can transmit life and death within a single encounter. The pervasive presence of reproductive en-ergy in all our explicitly religious rites demonstrates the difficulty of discerning life-giving from life-shattering power. The ancient fertility gods demonstrate how basic this connection is in our development as creatures. The Biblical prophetic tradition railed against these gods in a way which our age seems to have reduced to a struggle between ma-triarchy and patriarchy. The continuing wreckage of misplaced sexuality indicates there may have been - and may continue to be - something more primary at stake in the prophet's concern than merely preserving male privilege.

One epiphany of Venus is through the masks of Misogyny and Mishomony. As the names imply, Venus can become incarnate through the degradation, brutalization and hatred of a single sex. The physical results of misogyny are grimly visible in any daily newspaper. The fact that the results of Mishomony are seldom reported, and therefore less visible, does not make it less serious. Fractured self-esteem cripples a person and deeply affects their future relationships, regardless of the sex of the recipient of the abuse. Sadism, with its strident paranoia and lust for power fuels these epiphanies of Venus-driven fundamentalism.

Another epiphany of Venus is through the mask of sexual pleasure. Made incarnate in our culture through easy sexual encounters and the pervasive use of sexuality to sell everything from cars to deodorant, sexual pleasure promises us some facet of a 'better life' if only we follow or purchase whatever is being offered at the moment. The tragedies of AIDS, pregnant teenagers, guilt torn refugees from abortion clinics and the *ennui* of the empty Playboy Mansion speaks of Venus' fundamental barrenness. She is unable to deliver what she promises, although the recognition of her as a still-born savior comes only once the damage is done.

The primary dilemma in naming the bondage we may feel toward this implicit god is the painful recognition that the very force which creates life is at the core of our destructive actions. It is terrifying to recognize that life and death may be genetically identical realities. It may be easy to describe the *dynamics* of denial but it is very difficult to recognize and leave behind the *behavior* (rites) that cause chronic pain for ourselves and those we profess to care about.

No compendium of implicit deities would be complete without mentioning Mars, the god of war. Whether in the production of weapons of mass destruction or in the daily rattle of urban gunfire, this god consumes the resource of our planet and our soul. Mars is a voracious deity who appeals to our fundamental desire for power. Mars tempts us to believe that we have the strength to scale the very towers of heaven and impose our will upon them. Mars authorizes us to slay our neighbors once we believe they would deny us access to whatever the riches of heaven and earth may be. Mars draws strength from the very real and unfortunate brutality of our neighbors (tyrants of *all* political persuasions really do murder millions). One need only read the awful

account of a nation's progress into any war to be reminded of how the
same myopia can infect both sides in a conflict.[57] The scarred earth,
devastated psyches, crippled bodies and mass graves bear grim witness
to the *fascinocium* of Mars.

Mars woos us to death in the service of some greater cause. That the
cause may indeed be a just one, a goal worthy of self-sacrifice and
neighbor-murder only increases the need for wise discernment. The
soldier preparing to enter battle or to grant a desperately wounded
friend's request for relief can find his deliberations clouded by questions of an operation's worthiness. The Persian Gulf War reminds us
how the general question of a war's worthiness can personally impact a
family seeking pastoral support while their son, daughter, mother or
father is actually serving in harm's way. Few images more graphically
depict the wrenching nature of the rites of Mars that the site of *moth-
ers* in BDU's leaving behind their children. Few things illustrate our
blindness to the long-term impact of this rite on our culture than those
who toast such a rite as women finally coming of age.

We learn to worship Mars early, at baseball diamonds and skating
rinks, where we can easily forget that our children are playing a game.
Like other implicit deities, naming Mars as the one controlling our
lives allows us to assess his role in our life and evaluate our commitment to his ends. Even the people of God have called upon Mars more
than once to serve our own ends.

"My name is Legion"

We come finally to secular deities. One of the more promising lines
of current empirical research attempts to link explicit personality
disorders with specific configurations of religious belief. This research
draws upon the Million personality theory and a concept called
"theopathology." A diagnostic instrument is available from the author
of the research. The use of such an instrument could easily be
incorporated into the assessment process and notations on this
schema's **Axis II.** [58]

The underlying premise of this line of research underscores the
strong relationship between religious belief patterns and permanent
personality structures.[59] Sometimes we name these patterns in explicitly religious ways. We support them with religious rites or with the

tyranny of our own family history. Gathering information on the explicit impact of such religion can be handled by incorporating a religious history into the initial assessment phase of work with a person. Writing in this cited volume, Ana-Maria Rizzuto notes the following: "the taking of a religious history provides its richest information when it focuses on personal psychodynamics by attending to the beliefs the person has about herself or himself as a specific individual facing the divinity and human existence."[60] This is true regardless of the religious orientation of the caregiver.

For people afflicted with one of the personality disorders, the reality is that for many persons the anguish inherent in their pain has serious consequences for their emotional health, theological orientation and religious practice. Recent clinical studies which detail the social trauma which produces Post-Traumatic Stress Disorder with the development of Borderline Personality Disorder in a certain percentage of the population underscores the complex relationship between external events and our internal personality structure.[61] The interface between such events, our personality structure and our religious beliefs is no less complicated. The religiously oriented caregiver may need to become familiar with this research. The secular caregiver can no longer ignore the impact of religious belief and practice on a client and still believe they are providing effective care.[62]

These cloaked deities acquire social as well as personal dimensions. Thus the Power or Throne which may be violating the one who sits within our office may also be clouding our own vision of the literal as well as the sacred landscape. These are the deities of secular religion which seek cover under the prevailing *geist* of our culture. These are the gods of our particular sub-culture or nation who appear in benign guise but whose havoc can be extensive.

Religious caregivers most often concern themselves with the pain of an individual or family. But the pastoral way of viewing others is rooted in acknowledging the covenant between the individual and the wider community. What may we do if those who appear in our office, or before the communion rail, are gripped by a deity who rules an entire city? To what diagnostic rubric do we turn to discern the wounds left by a broken culture? What avenues of healing are available to those whose lives are cursed and crushed by Thrones and Principalities which shape the destiny of an entire people? Here we must be willing to discern the secular religion which bids us to sell our spiritual birth-right for the security of social acceptance and national security.[63]

Conclusion

Our various nations invoke founding deities, whether they appear in primal myth or incarnate as historical founders. In times of crisis we appeal to their memory. We mark their birthdays as holy days of special celebration. We enshrine them in public temples of government and our debate over those shrines can be protracted and shrill as our debate over placing F. D. R. in a wheelchair or adding kneeling nurses and standing combat figures to the Vietnam Memorial area amply illustrate. We cast their names upon our boulevards and populate our parks with the their statues. Whether explicit, implicit or purely secular, there is a religious dimension to personal and social practices which shape our hearts and behavior.[64]

These are not necessarily misdirected practices. But as with all other gods, we are often oblivious to their life-shaping power. Or we overemphasize their life-giving contributions. Sometimes the terror these gods evoke is the terror which comes from being an oppressed cultural group. Sometimes the adoration these gods engender is one arising from the gratitude of liberation. More than one society has revolted against the extant gods because they failed to deliver the cargo of life and liberty. Such events may be outside of the ethos of a 50 minute clinical hour. But they are not outside of the prophetic concern of pastors and the religious community.

Chapter 5

Feeling Terror or Rage

"Who are you to question my wisdom with your ignorant, empty words? Stand up now like a man and answer the questions I ask you."[65] Here we have a fully formed theophany of the Deity, expressing primal Otherness toward a solitary member of our species. Small wonder that despite the majestic poetry of the passages which follow, Job's response is one of total acquiescence.[66] He returns to the faith whereupon a beneficent Deity rewards him with "even more" blessings than he first enjoyed (v. 12). In the interim, he does acknowledge that the event has been transforming (v. 5). The Book of Job details his travail through the emotions of terror and rage as he discovers the limits of his own power. As important as this discovery may be in religious care, the more primary issue of the heart is the awesome recognition that the god one has worshipped not only has limits but apparently intends to wound the faithful! This is indeed a god "whom I talked about but did not understand" (v. 3).

When the Ground of our Being shakes beneath our feet, we feel a mixture of terror and rage. Like the soldier cringing in a bunker during an artillery barrage, such terror is an appropriate response to realistic threat. When the barrage concludes, there arises in the heart a compelling desire to strike back. *Hard!* These emotions are compounded when the shaking comes from One whose greatness we admired, whose strength formerly gave us shelter and whose calmness may have invited us to stand close. Our neighbors may experience our anxiety or depression. Our family members may know the vigilance of our terror and the slash of our rage. But for the one who has been betrayed by their god, the feelings of terror and rage are the red and

black hurricane warning banners hoisted into the gale at the center of
the soul.

There are many conditions a caregiver encounters where someone's
basic trust of another has been betrayed. Divorces, forced retirements,
natural disasters and catastrophic illness certainly provide ready examples of such betrayals. In spite of our best preparations these events
can be terrifying. We desire our world to be predictable and safe for
ourselves and those we care about. This is more than a desire. We
believe this is our *entitlement*. We do not *deserve* to get AIDS. We do
not *deserve* to find our wife in the arms of another. We do not *deserve*
to have the river wash away our home. It is not *fair* to watch the cas-
ket of our son disembark from a military transport.

Try as we might to calm the post-disaster nightmares, the memories
may echo whenever we hear the wind whistle or the boss clear her
throat. Somehow the mantra "I know that life isn't fair" fails to express our rage or help us reclaim the Holy. We long for the Greatest
Grandfather to tell us about the good old days or to hold us secure
against the night.

Our feelings of terror have their roots in the ancient formulas of
blessings and curses which undergird every religion. Gods demand
followers who adore them. Believers who express the appropriate adoration and faithfulness are promised the blessings of prosperity and
health (cargo). Gods may destroy followers who leave them for other
gods, spread nasty rumors about them or who are generally disobedi-
ent. Thus to leave a god is to run the terrifying risk of being on the
receiving end of a curse. Ancient myths are full of such stories and
our nightmares give urgent power to such terrors.

Yet our various gods fail us! We feel abandoned or singled out for
special tragedy. When these failings occur we can find a way to explain their failure through a system of theodicy. But if a god's failures
are persistent or their blessings are unsatisfying, we may finally feel
compelled to abandon the god. Abandoning a god who has failed a be-
liever inevitably involves destroying the deity. Thus iconoclastic rage
becomes the converted back side of devotion to the icon. Conversions
and new vocations may ultimately blossom from such a firestorm. But
first comes the dark night of the soul. Reformations and the pro-
nouncements of great church councils may be the ultimate institutional
result of such demythologizing and restructuring. But their elder sib-
lings are Ghost Dances and Inquisitions.

The immediate implications for both religious and secular clinician are that these dynamics of terror and rage may likely be present whenever there is a situation of betrayal or isolation. Our presence may evoke these deep feelings, seemingly unbidden by our action but more by our representative (counter-transferential) status. If we have the presence of mind and grace of spirit to remain secure in the face of such terror and soothing in the swirling firestorm which destroys the idol, then we offer the opportunity for the person to reclaim the Holy. These are the continuing tasks for religious diagnosis and care on **Axis II.**

Receiving the Terror and Withstanding the Rage

"You white folks just don't understand," he said with quiet forcefulness. "When you *invite* us. . . . when you try to get me to say 'I am angry,' you have no idea what you are asking me to say." There was a palpable pause. The supervisor could hear the swirl of feelings welling up from the core of a long buried memory.

"I saw a Black man *hanged* because he told a White man he was *ANGRY!* I was in the first grade! What a horrible thing to see!"

His sentences punctured the veil of time. For a brief moment in that small room you could once again hear the lurid screams of that White mob. You could smell the terrified sweat of its running victim. His voice trembled as he concluded, "I *remember* that day to this very *moment*. . . and I. . . AM. . . ANGRY!"

Expressing this depth of remembered terror does not come quickly or easily with the counseling relationship. The perfunctory post-sermon greeting at the church doorway or the six session confines of managed psychological care do not provide an environment secure enough in which to unleash, let alone explore, this power. This is not to say that the preacher is insulated from the ripples of such rage or that the clinician is unaware of the depth of inexpressible terror. But one must feel supremely secure with the caregiver before daring to risk words which might invite the retaliation of the very gods. This is truly profanity, for such words rupture a deeply held but destructive covenant. It is the defining profanity of a wounded soul beginning the quest to recover the Holy.

We are a culture which seems voyeristically obsessed with terror and rage. The writings of Stephen King and the latest incarnation of *The Predator* may focus our attention on contrived scenes of terror. The celluloid shadows of rage flit upon each season's blow-'em-up movies. Yet while vigorously demanding the right to produce and view these intense violations of body and soul via fantasy, we seem unable to form relationships which are secure enough to help one another move beyond genuine violations. We have come to expect that such betrayals may be adequately resolved within the confines of a 145 minute movie. The pastoral relationship is one of the few remaining professional settings which allow for adequate time in which the soul can begin to approach a depthful and complete addressing of the wounding, sacrifices, terror and rage which form the core identity of the gods whom we serve. Certainly taking on the gods requires more trust in your companion and guide than a solitary weekend workshop or the twice-a-year perfunctory holiday visit.

How does a religious clinician receive or evoke such terror? Can we safely allow genuine rage to surface outside the confines of a psychiatric hospital? A pastor's self-understanding is crucial to such evocation. We must rediscover the core of a pastoral identity which accepts the caregiving relationship as one in which the pastor represents the Holy One who "protects me from the power of death."[67] Because the pastor stands with another as an agent of the One who "will not abandon (me) to the world of the dead," each relationship has within it the potential for such safe disclosure. The pastor is more than a non-rejecting mirror who empathically nurtures a splintered introject of the personality. The pastor symbolizes much more than the talk show hostess whose daily parade of the wounded among us is titillating but ultimately non-healing.

Having said these things, I would hasten to add that empathy is also an absolutely necessary ingredient in evoking another's terror and rage. Empathy is a process in which the caregiver does not merely understand another's suffering and dilemma. Empathy is a decided step toward or walking with another. This is hard to accomplish with someone who feels their entire life has been one of violation and betrayal. Using the words "terror" and "betrayal" in a judicious, directive fashion forms a depthful empathic bridge with such persons. This language may be difficult for the counselor (religious or secular) to utilize if she has not made peace with her own feelings of violation. It is difficult for the caregiver who must have everyone like her to be frustrating enough with another to evoke their rage. Standing alongside someone terrified at the prospect of leaving an inadequate god may be difficult but it does reimburse the counselor's efforts with a feeling of benign power. It is satisfying to be protective of another person. It is much more problematic to withstand the rage of someone who has identified us projectively as a primary source of their anguish. This virulent rage seems to boil up without warning from the very depth of a private Hell. For a period of time the caregiver as the person they know themself to be *ceases to exist* in the psyche of the counselee. In "our" place the individual or couple "sees," incarnate, the very one who has produced the primary disruption in his or her life.

The major personality disorders and the results of historic drug dependence are the primary categories where the pastor should be alert for such strong eruptions. It is important to remember that the person is trying to destroy a *god* even if the deity is manifested only through the epiphany of alcohol, the natural response of a frustrated employer or the client's misperception of a long-suffering spouse.

Sometimes the "god" that is left behind is an enmeshing parent or social structure. This destructuring causes great anxiety for all concerned. In writing about this process within Jewish families, Howard Cooper notes, "the over-enmeshment of Jewish families can mean that parents, while consciously wishing for their children's success and independence, may unconsciously fear or resent or envy that same independence. Feelings of emptiness or rejection or anger can be hard to acknowledge when one is supposed to want all the best for them."[68] Obviously the counselor will need to position himself in such a way as to avoid replicating this anxiety within the family, whether the client is the parent or the separating member of the next generation. The linkage between this rather natural process and clinical realities is underscored by Cooper, for he notes that "sometimes the anger at the smothering expectations of parents becomes directed by the child. . ..against themselves. This leads to depressions, the eating problems and disorders, the use and abuse of tranquillisers, alcohol or drugs and the psychosomatic complaints that have become so prevalent in Anglo-Jewry."[69]

The provider of care can withstand the rage by taking several steps. First, the pastor or clinician needs to retain an attachment to the dam-

aged inward child whose hurt at the betrayal is what fuels the god-de-
stroying rage. Second, the effective care provider must retain an out-
ward posture of non-reactive detachment. When these two relational
dynamics are balanced effectively the individual will feel empathically
cared for but will not overly objectify *you* as their latest tormentor. A
third factor which is helpful in withstanding this level of rage is to di-
lute the rage via group treatment. Whether this is achieved through an
explicitly therapeutic group such as Narcotics Anonymous or an im-
plicitly therapeutic-educational group like the Young Adult's Bible
Class, the effect can be the same. A group can help an individual
overcome the isolation which appears to be inherent in this level of
pain while at the same time providing a more corporate *persona* to ab-
sorb the projected hurt. A single person does not become the target of
the projection and thus no single other person is overwhelmed. Finally, pastoral clinicians particularly must recognize that in this area
of the soul a person may sense, if not always fully recognize, that the
Terrifying Darkness which has betrayed them is not simply Another
but in some fundamental fashion is also a part of the Self. Recognizing this dynamic early in the caring relationship can help the counselor understand the depth of anguish a person may be containing as
well as alert the counselor to take seriously the possibilities of homicide or suicide. Remember, the person is seeking to destructure a *god*.

Symbolizing the Terror and Rage

When my oldest son was two years old we were walking through the
twisting hallways of Chicago's Natural History Museum. Somewhere
in the Tibetan display we rounded the corner to be confronted by the
life-sized statue of a fierce god. We were startled! Except that where
my ego immediately over-rode my fear with the message *"statue* of Tibetan god; harmless," his ego said "RUN!" He ran straight into my
arms!

We all need some way of naming or symbolizing the forces which
terrify and enrage us. While distress at this level often becomes focused on a series of realistic betrayals to which therapeutic attention
must legitimately be directed, deeper therapeutic work begins once the
person identifies the factors in their life which compelled them to be
positioned into a posture of vulnerability and betrayal. Two of the
most common ways for these forces to be symbolized is through the

Devouring Female and the Overshadowing Male.[70] Such inward symbolizations may lead a person to search out the safety of intimacy with a series of companions who will finally be the god one has always wanted; yet, in each case these chosen gods inevitably seem to confirm the projections of devouring and overshadowing realities. Clinicians readily identify this compulsive repetition's psychological dimensions, for we see it written large upon the twisted limbs of many family trees. Counselors may also find it fruitful to attend to the spiritual dimensions of such painful quests. The spiritual dynamics fueling these patterns can run the symbolic gamut from being uncomfortable with male/female pronouns for God to something much more sinister and complex.

The first task of diagnostic inquiry for this **Axis** is to acquire a complete and realistic history of the person's broken covenants and betrayers. A multi-generational family history can give names and faces to individuals and settings in which covenants of safety were broken. Such a detailed accounting begins the healing process by giving an objective focus for otherwise unfocused feelings. While an affective focus of care can help debreed the wounds of betrayal and establish a bond of healing empathy, a cognitive focus in our religious conversations can help delimit the boundaries of the actual betrayal(s). The Socratic method of eliciting such information, gently illustrated by Aaron Beck and others, shows how these two approaches can be effectively combined. When these elements of caring work in tandem, the suffering person has both a genuine place upon which to focus their quest for healing as well as having access to the true core of their hurt.

But so often, as it was with Job cited earlier, our experience of betrayal appears to go much deeper than mere family history. By the time these broken covenants are acknowledged we have built portions of our lives around them. They have assumed the status of the gods within us in function if not always in name. We believe we cannot live without them, or at least we recognize that to try living without them will significantly alter who we are. Here we no longer have the addiction or the personality pattern. The addiction has us. We are the personality disorder.

It is here in this second **Axis** of diagnostic inquiry that the religious counselor is on home soil. By our inclination and training we have both access to the names of the gods as well as the authority to defuse their curses. This was brought home to me in a rather forceful way by two parallel clinical settings. The first came as some area clinicians working with combat veterans began to encounter men who spoke about their angels. The second is the renewed dialogue within clinical and research circles about the topics of demon possession and victimization by Satanic cults. Each of these discussions would have been dismissed out of hand a decade ago, due primarily to an overly positivistic view of the psyche. But in a world which remains hungry for mythic reality, such symbolizations have returned to currency.[71] Each topic has been broached with me by competent clinicians who were struggling to understand the depth of their clients' realities as well as search for personal ways to understand the depth of distress they were encountering. The ontology of such forces may be a matter for reasoned theological debate. However, in the consulting room and confessional, the pastor's most helpful stance is to assist the person in naming the confronting terror. Here we have the rich spiritual resources of historic pastoral care at our disposal. We would be well served to become reacquainted with these resources, for no other healing discipline has been charged with their preservation and prescription.

Calming the Terror and Redirecting the Rage

The provider of religious care has some resources which are both effective and immediately at hand. The first resource a pastor has is the cry of lament. A full-throated lament is quite different from self-centered whining. A lament calls us to help the person construct a bill of particulars against God. This act combines the emotional release so necessary for healing as well as enlists a cognitive structure which deals responsibly with genuine religious reconstruction. A second resource is to guide the person through an introduction to alternative names for God. This is not as easy as it sounds. This step certainly needs to go beyond merely replacing pronouns to be truly effective. The pastor or counselor may wish to suggest alternative images for God and utilize them in corporate worship as a way of circumventing the re-traumatization which happens to some when only traditional names for God are used. Unfortunately the early attempts at inclusive liturgies often created as much distress as they appeared to resolved. This intervention must be crafted with great care. It is satisfying to calm another's terror. It is much more problematic, and not always fully successful, when we try to redirect another's rage. Too often we settle for giving them something or someone else with whom to be rageful. It is an arduous task to sublimate personal betrayal into a healing alternative. Thus we may see a certain type of hurting person who has gone from one *cause celeb* to another. They always seem to be hot on the trail of the latest villain. But they do not seem to be truly at peace with themselves. They may not be able to bring reconciliation into the world which they see in such desperate need, primarily because the truly desperate need is for their own inner peace.

Such was the case for Paul, mentioned earlier. The more he railed against "those red necked boys with the Jeeps and dogs," the more obvious his isolation became. As his efforts to identify pedophiles intensified, the more brittle his righteousness became. Ulcers and high blood pressure quickly become the visible *stigmata* of the gods whom he longed to destroy. A more healthy pattern of sublimating the rage of early wounding or repeated losses into a redemptive effort is seen in candidates for the various helping professions, including clergy.[72], [73]

Conclusion

As a concluding comment, let me mention several resources where such redirection can occur. A directed Ignatian retreat or involvement in the Cursillio movement can assist someone in finding an explicitly religious framework into which to mold her emerging religious sentiment. Involvement with a spiritual director can be another fruitful avenue for some people. There are numerous avenues of spiritual exploration which range from the intensely private to the very public. All will have some efficacy for some people. The pastoral task here is to discern the ones which are most likely to be helpful to the person who has come to us for care.

Chapter 6

Recovering the Hope of Ultimacy

"It's an old table I inherited from my Mother
It stood in my kitchen
Scowling with its varnished-over-varnished-over eye
Saying, 'Go Ahead! I dare you!'"

I remember her poem, which came unbidden after more than five years of friendship. For years it seemed we wandered through the layers of her parental varnish. Each new layer of betrayal or failure of care only seemed to take her deeper into her grief. Few flaws within the congregation escaped her rage. People said she was "shy" but the trembling hands on the guitar disclosed terror.

So I gave it to a friend whose patient stripping
Rubbed into it the beauty its Maker had intended,"

The poem concluded with these lines after she had met a companion with whom to share her life. Together they began searching for a new church. She had matured enough to not only recognize the limits of affection which another could offer, but she could also begin loving herself. Her journey of discovery with her spouse and her faith community has continued. She has learned to celebrate the gifts which exist within her congregation without expecting unbending doctrinal constancy or unfailing corporate piety.

Neither the fashionable existentialism of America's 1960's nor the grim atheism of Europe's 1930's has withstood our primary human need for an Ultimate Concern[74] The renewed spiritual hunger

49

sweeping the world in the 1990's testifies to the intensity of our need for a Divine Object. If we are fortunate, we will discover the God Who Looks For Us. We will find another who faithfully sustains a covenant of unswerving love (*agape*). If we have not learned from our journey towards healing, we will encounter the God Who Looks Like Us. We will be devoured or overpowered by one more deity made in the image of our own desperately unmet needs. The tragedies of cults as disparate as Heaven's Gate and the Branch Davidians are current testimonies to the virulence of these devouring gods. We may attach ourselves to a community of hope which is moving expectantly toward the future. We may also find yet another community whose spiritual center reinforces our nightmares and aggravations. Wherever religious professionals serve they will encounter people at various points in this journey. Clinicians of both secular and sacred stripe must carry out the tasks of diagnosis (naming the pain and guiding the care) with those who invite us to walk beside them in this quest for a satisfying, life-sustaining God.

Grieving the Loss of Ultimacy

He can remember sitting in the Reception Center at Ton San Nuht. "I heard three chaplains talking. Two seasoned ones were leaving for the States, and they were talking to the new one coming in country. The older ones were in despair about the condition of the troops and their own loss of faith. One man told the new chaplain, who would be his replacement, 'let me set you up with my housekeeper. She can *really* take care of you!' When the new chaplain's shock registered on them, the other chaplain said to the new one, 'don't worry. You'll lose whatever faith you came over here with," he continued. "I remember thinking how awful it was to overhear that conversation. I remember wondering, 'where have I landed myself, if the chaplains are losing their faith?' " he concluded.

There would be other failures of pastoral care during his year in Vietnam and future Army career. Those would be bitter and dark years but they would not be empty years. Even in his disappointments there was the implicit recognition that life was meant to be more than the grim amoral anguish so common to many soldiers of his time. These experiences drove home to him the truth that the God he needed was not to be found within either military life or the formal religious structures of his childhood faith. When he recognized that this absence did not mean the death of God, but only the death of the god who looked like himself, his journey out of the depths took an upward turn.

Soothing the Loss of Attachment

While it is painful to recognize that we are not whom we thought ourselves to be, it is devastating to acknowledge the god we have built our life around has vanished. We might laugh in better times about the image of God who says "I ain't the one who's moved," but the internal experience is no laughing matter. Whether our god has been explicit, implicit or fully secular, we feel completely unattached and adrift. This is a loss which must be soothed. Whether we are soothed through therapy, worship, friendship or social attachment, this sense of loss can be healed. Religious counselors and the community of faith can play a primary role in this healing process.

Whether we run away from or destroy the God Who Looks Like Us, there is a loss which must be grieved. We speak glibly about a person's loss of faith, but one does not buy faith at the local 7-Eleven. We may worry at another's loss of hope, but hope does not spring up nearly as easily as a new crop of Spring dandelions. Most often the grieving process will carry counselor and person back through many significant spiritual landmarks.[75] These need not be religious memories but they will be memories of events, places and persons with whom we shared a touch of the Divine. This grieving is not something a person can do in their spare time or on a single weekend retreat. Even though the person may look outwardly well, their inner attention will be focused upon this primary wound.

So what are the words and rites which can assist in the healing journey? As mentioned earlier, the words of lament can soothe the wounded heart. General laments, like temper tantrums, come easily to the lips. Specific laments, which lay out the explicit disappointments, betrayals and terrors are much more difficult to compose. Yet the counselor or pastor can assist in this step by empathically mirroring the loss of ultimacy and the desire for God to be other than what one has experienced.

Thus when the young man noted in the introduction finally got to wondering where *was* the God Who Protects Innocent Children, I said "You really ache because God was not there to shield you."

The choice of the word *ache* is not accidental. Ache identifies the deep loss of ultimacy and assists the person in recovering their rage. Once recovered, the rage can be redirected. As the rage is redirected toward an appropriate object (in this case the absent deity), the ache and rage can be soothed and healed. Until such soothing occurs, rages can only be repetitively felt and all too often expressed only in destructive fashions.

Sometimes the ultimacy which is lost is an express betrayal of religious belief. For example, I recall a pastor who sheltered an abused woman in his home. One Sunday evening there was an explosion in the stairway which led from their apartment to the street. A wall of flame erupted along with the strong smell of gasoline. The woman's husband was later convicted of arson.

While everyone escaped harm and the fire was contained, several of the pastor's religious beliefs were lost in the ashes. He had to review his belief in the Almighty's unconditional protection. He had to face a level of evil in another which did not easily give way to his compassion. He also had to acknowledge his own strong desire to retaliate. This desire, with the emotional aftermath, compelled him to grieve the loss of the pacifistic god he had been preaching about.

To his credit, he took the time and energy necessary to do the theological and emotional grieving. The event remains a touchstone of his preaching and his continued spiritual growth. Although he retains the pacifism of his denomination (a historic Peace Church), he is much more empathic toward those whose impulse of self-defense prompts the use of measured force where before he had only words of uncompromising critique. Discovering the depths of good and evil usually requires that we leave our Garden of Eden.[76]

Identifying what or who one has lost is important. But soothing the wound of detachment also requires a recognition of what *remains* of the disappointing object. Thus when we begin coming to terms with our parents' failures or seek to discover a more satisfying adult religious faith, genuine healing comes as the continued blessings of our heritage are identified. While the individual's natural dynamic of repression tends to bury hurriedly their losses so that only the strengths remain, the clinician may wish to direct attention toward these remaining benefits. Worship services typically include songs of praise and prayers of thanksgiving. These can draw our attention to the breadth of religious sentiment when we are personally overwhelmed with a specific grief. Thus my friend's table remained in her kitchen. She truly did refin--ish it and, eventually, hosted her mother there for a holiday meal. While her mother remained much as my friend remembered from childhood, she no longer looked to her mother as the primary source of her worth.

Releasing the Expectation of Constancy

A major shock in our loss of ultimacy is the recognition that the deity we have built our life around has changed. Grief over an unanswered prayer for healing, terror at being unprotected, and rage billowing up from a devastating catastrophe all have one thing in common. We demand God treat us in a very predictable and constant fashion. God does not. The longer we live, the more we come to recognize that only a very few things are truly constant. None of the constants involve our life with other people or the Person God Is. [77]

Living in a world where few things are truly constant can prompt the nightmares or social predations of unalloyed psychosis. Only a small number of counselors and a minuscule number of pastors will encounter this level of distress in others. We are much more likely to be called upon to assist someone in sorting through the murky boundary between the distressing "constancy" within their own family and their variant experiences in the wider culture.

I recall one person whom I have seen in a clinical setting for several years. Within a family of several males, he has always been the unfavored one. Neither oldest nor youngest nor judged most handsome, he has been content to accomplish several tasks on his own: completing college, completing a professional training program, purchasing his own cars, working two jobs and remaining free from crushing debt. Because of his constant experience of critique by his family, he still initially hears internal criticism for his achievements. His primary internal response to a new setting is to flinch, even when those around him are applauding. He has had a difficult time releasing himself from the expectation of constant critique.

What has been helpful in caregiving conversation with him? First, to invite out and even embellish the genuine litany of critique by his family. Inviting him to disclose the dregs of his anguish has afforded the opportunity for emotional release. Embellishment of the critique by the counselor has compelled him to accurately state the degree of critique. This also involves him in the meta-message that at least one authority figure (a counselor) may be resisted without the experience of rejection. Second, to invite him to reflect on what is unique about the counseling relationship. His words fall generally in the area of "but you are different" or "but this is a different relationship." He is correct, which leads to the third step: asking him to detail how this relationship is different and how this difference affects him. Once completed, I have encouraged him to slowly find other people or relationships in which he has felt the same way.

The net effect of this process, which spanned over six years, was his discovery of competing constancy's. There is a set of constants within his family of origin - to be sure! But these are not the sole constancy's around him. There are many others whose constants includes affirmation and celebration of his value.

This may seem like a simple process. It is. It can also be painstakingly slow if the person's need for security is high. His contemporary struggles to discern what was expected within an office or a class always surfaced multiple memories of past critiques. It seemed that each of these had to be identified, raged about, trembled over and then grieved. Only then could he begin to *hear* the new affirmation which might be present for him in the new setting. The emotional and spiritual process is similar in complexity to the physical task of learning how to feed yourself or walk after a major stroke.

His most recent task has been to search for a church. Within the rubrics of a narrow theology, his search is not about "being saved." He is only approaching the place where he may hear a message of spiritual hope. But within a more encompassing view, it seems to me that he illustrates precisely what is meant by *prevenient grace*, the grace of God which searches us out before we even know we need grace. For someone with his past experience, even this news will be something which will challenge the old constancy's.

This situation mirrors the dilemmas faced by many people. They are among us in terror, rage and grief over an ultimacy which has fundamentally betrayed them. Their memory of betrayal hampers them from forming new attachments with significant others and with new communities. Pastors and counselors can be part of the team which guides others to more satisfying and nurturing attachments. But we will be effective only as we understand the degree of risk which the person perceives they must undertake in truly releasing the patterns which have guided them for years.

Rediscovering the Hope of Ultimacy

He stood before us in the sand-colored BDU's of desert camouflage. "When we left for the Gulf," he said, "You Tet Vets promised you would support us. You promised you would not let happen to us what happened to you. I stand before you today to say 'Thank You!' You kept your promise!"

The speaker, a veteran of both Vietnam and the Persian Gulf War, went on to detail the impact of letter writing campaigns and homecoming celebrations on the soldiers who returned from the Persian Gulf. "In most cases, when we looked to see who was the person behind the scenes who organized the effort, we discovered it was a Vietnam veteran. We weren't surprised. We *are* appreciative!"

It was an electrifying moment. I could not tell whose eyes had the most tears in them, his or ours. What we were all experiencing during those heady days immediately after our comrades came home was the rediscovery of the hope of love. We were rediscovering the hope of ultimacy. So often when a god dies, what dies is not just love but also the *hope* that love and ultimacy will ever be found again. Whether the dying god is explicit, implicit or secular, one has the sense of losing a fundamental anchor. Yet upon the road toward a new god whose identity is more adequate to our needs, one must rediscover the hope of love and ultimacy. One must experience being found by the Ultimate One and become capable, again, of responding to the Ultimate One.

Job is the Biblical narrative for grieving the loss of ultimacy and the rediscovery of awe. But it is the Song of Songs which celebrates the hope of loving, passionate ultimacy. Both volumes are powerfully written although they are only single examples of a wider religious literature addressing these fundamental human themes. They weave together the affects of terror, rage, passion, and joy with the aesthetics of a well constructed spiritual intellect. In doing so these documents model the road to rediscovering hope for the wounded heart. The religious affirmation is that one can rediscover hope, love and ultimacy. It is a part of the counselor's task to assist others in this delicate but arduous journey.

Negotiating with the Almighty One

This sounds like the ultimate in arrogance. One at once pictures the trembling Alice "the small and meek" before the Wizard of Oz, "the great and powerful." There is clearly more to the Deity than just someone behind a curtain. We must approach and negotiate with the One Who Cradles the Stars. We must replace the God Who Looks Like Us with a living encounter between ourselves and the God Who Looks For Us.[78] If the Biblical narrative is any clue, God appears to be familiar with treaty negotiations[79] and not just with curses.[80] Merle Jordan is correct when he asserts that the task of pastors is to train people to "take on the gods."[81]

"I watched the mortars walk up toward the rock where I was hiding. I saw Death! He was taking souls! I remember hollerin' "I ain't askin' much God, just be with me now and I'm all yours," he would recall later when asked how he came to feel God's call to ministry. As much as we may snicker about the results of such foxhole negotiations with God, they compose a significant strata in human religious experience.[82]

Sometimes the negotiating involves an enhanced understanding of our medical needs in the face of our belief in personal invulnerability. Sometimes the negotiating must address the boundary of genuine hope in the midst of grievous suffering. At times the contract to be rewritten is the expectations between family members or spouses. But at each point there comes the moment when one *must* face a confrontation with the Force that bears down upon us. It is a task of the pastoral caregiver to legitimate the right of a person to negotiate with such a Force and to direct them toward the resources which will aid them in this task. Sometimes it falls to the pastor to be the one leading the negotiations. This is the heart of the shamanistic task. This is the core of intercessory prayer.

The boundary between negotiating, religious ritual and magic is ambiguous at best. All three religious traditions go back at least to our Proto-Neolithic roots.[83] What these three share in common is the recognition of human dependency and divine sufficiency in the face of identified human need. Where they differ is the degree of compulsion which the act seeks to exert upon both parties. With ritual and outright magic there is the assumption that the Deity *must* act in a prescribed fashion due to the accurate behavior of the religiously faithful. With mature negotiation there is an enhanced ability for the person to state needs in a forceful manner with the expectation that God *may* grant the request. Often the pastoral, clinical task is limited to walking with the person as they make their way through the thicket of understanding which separates these two points of view.

To negotiate with the Force which bears down upon us is an act of hope. When we negotiate we express the hope in God's lovingkindness *(hesed)* and faithfulness *(pistos)* towards us or toward those whose names are written upon our hearts. Pastors and counselors can model mature negotiating skills for people by the way we offer public prayers and our private bedside intercessions. We can also invite members of a congregation to join in such prayers, called *bidding prayers,* as well as making provision for our counseling visits to include times in which prayer is a shared experience.[84]

Beyond these ritual actions, pastors can translate the skills and attitudes associated with assertiveness training into one's posture toward God. A part of the Good News is not just that God seeks to save humanity from our brokenness but that God desires us to be responsible and responsive partners in a new covenant.[85] In the end it is the outcome of such negotiations which influence us in the direction of terror, rage or renewed faith. In terms of the courage and skill needed to conduct such negotiations it matters little whether the Force we wrestle with is the Mother who bore us, the Family which surrounded us, the Nation which called us to duty, the Church which taught us or an epiphany of God Almighty in the still small voice or whirlwind.[86] . If one is to truly resolve the betrayals which underline the anguish in this region of the heart, the god made in our image must be identified, its shortcomings acknowledged and a new covenant forged.

Receiving the Spirit

The structures and forces which shape our lives are more than mere mental constructs. Just as a city is more than a collection of varied architectural styles so the human heart is more than a collage of varied values. Giving up or tearing down one of the gods who has formed our life requires tremendous effort. Yet without something to take its place, the emptiness in our heart is worse than whatever demon may have lived there before.[87] We long for a new source of life, even if what is planted in our lives is a patch of wildflowers.

Thus the final step in the counseling effort here, on this **Axis**, is to guide the person or family toward a new discovery of love or an experience of God's living grace. This may take many forms and, on the surface, it may appear to be a purely secular enterprise. But if the religious counselor truly believes that "nothing can separate us from the love of God"[88] then perhaps the corollary "my grace is sufficient for you"[89] is also true. Sometimes the sufficient grace is the renewing of marriage vows or the taking of an anti-depressant which allows sleep to finally come. Sometimes it is hearing the words of apology from a parent. Such acts are powerful in and of themselves. But they impact us with a spirit that sets some part of us free. It is precisely this newly forged freedom, unencumbered by the terrors of an inadequate god and not driven by the rage over a betraying god, which marks the rebirth of hope within the heart.[90]

The pastoral counseling task comes to bear as we draw attention to the person's emerging freedom. It is a much more effective intervention to wonder with the person if they can compare and contrast their present feelings and actions with those which consumed them three, six or nine months ago. My own experience is that often their face takes on a deeper glow, as if for the first time they recognize that they have truly come through at least a portion of their struggle. Allowing the person to identify and claim their growth, rather than us announcing their growth or exhorting their maturity, furthers the healing process. The person's discovery strengthens their ego's ability in self-assessment.

Conclusion

Thus far we have addressed the diagnostic areas of ethical and devotional need. In both areas the persons we care for will bring their strengths as well as their wounds. While the ethical need may be explicit and obvious, the devotional need is often implicit. The devotional need often requires much more attentiveness to discern as well as greater effort by all parties to resolve. There remains one area where religious diagnosis can be valuable. This is the existential dimension to human life. Here we shall attempt to name some of the deepest distress to which the human spirit is subject.

Part III:
Dread and the Feeling of Defilement

Chapter 7

Being Abandoned

You could hear the piano playing inside the church from outside the large, red double doors. Its chords penetrated the traffic noise. When I entered the sanctuary I recognized the muscular form bent over the keys. Although the music was not a song, it was a tuneful rendition of his inner world. Rhythmic. Forceful. Chaotic. Phrases of tenderness were followed hard by passages of violent urgency. I sat in the rear of the sanctuary. This was holy ground.

When his prayer was over, he rose and walked toward the rear of the sanctuary. His way of greeting was to ask me if I had seen one of the church members who was an attorney. "I'm going to sue the builders of the John Hancock Building and the Sears Tower," he said simply. "They heard my prophecy on North Avenue Beach and used it to plan their buildings. Now there are rich people living in the buildings I designed while I'm sleeping on the street."

Through the years he was a periodic visitor to the church. Sometimes he would rise during the middle of worship to ask a question. When he remembered to take his thorazine he enjoyed periods of lucidness. When he did not maintain himself in this way, violence and hospitalization would quickly overtake him. He seemed unaware of his effect on others, although he was perceptive about another person's ability to help or harm him. The details of his psychiatric and social history did not seem to matter nearly as much as his current experience of isolation and the court's demand of continued psychiatric care. Pastors and counselors periodically have the opportunity to sit with others whose brain and soul appear to be broken apart. It is not that all of these persons are intellectually marred or socially isolated. But their inward emotional experiences appear to set them apart. Some hold responsible social positions. Others are able to remain only marginally employed. Most do not seem to do exceptionally well in intimate relationships, whether in marriage or work. There appears to be an air of detachment about them which others find mildly to significantly troubling.

It is as though there is a coating of broken glass upon their life. Sometimes when the sunlight strikes the glass there is a refraction of light into a rainbow. But just as often the glass of their inner experience simply cuts upon those who draw close to them. More important for diagnostic purposes, such individuals seem to symbolize God in ways which depict an experience which is at once overwhelming and yet alienating, unreachable and yet persistently at hand, fundamentally confirming while at the same time evoking feelings of their being utterly damned. They give every appearance of attempting to hold life together through a bewildering series of disruptions which they seek to explain through a painful array of paradoxes.

For some of these individuals a psychiatric diagnosis of "paranoid schizophrenia" or "schizotypal personality" appears to be behaviorally descriptive. Yet for many others there is not a clear psychiatric nosology. We do not have a consistent religious way of assessing these individuals' religious life or gauging the pain which they bear . . . or which we perceive *ourselves* to be bearing if we were in their condition. Hearing their anguish and bringing some order to their pain is difficult for even skilled clinicians, regardless of theoretical orientation. Guiding the religious care of such a person is even more problematic, especially if the person is otherwise healthy and not in a hospital setting.

Defilement and the Experience of Profound Abandonment

The sharp stench of gasoline shook her awake! It was still dark in the box canyon where her attackers had brought her more than six hours ago. Her broken arm, ripped clothing and numerous wounds caused by the knives bore mute testimony to the violence of their assault. "We're gonna burn you like the garbage you are," snarled one of the men. Under the deep starlight of an Arizona sky she prepared to die. Later she would confide, "I don't know why they didn't kill me. I don't know what stopped them. But they argued among themselves for awhile and then left. I fainted again. Later I found a creek and washed myself in the water. Somehow I made it back to a main road and help."

"I feel so utterly unclean. I wonder who would ever want me. I hold myself at night and try to cry. But my tears are dry.

"I haven't been back to church. I feel so unworthy to be there. And I keep wondering. In that hell of a canyon, *where was God?!*"

Her words were a confession of abandonment and defilement. Her query is one echoed by multitudes of people whose suffering we, the sheltered, can hardly comprehend. Yet many of these who have suffered so grievously sit, walk and work among us. They are our wives, parents, brothers and bosses. In a previous generation we could identify some who had known such horrors, for they bore the tattoo of the Holocaust upon a forearm. Today the names of the tormentors differ. But the wounds they have left upon the human heart are well known by those called to be healers.

Whether etched upon the psyche a single slice at a time or impressed into the marrow during the grim Sarejevo winter, humans who undergo such deep suffering report a feeling of abandonment and defilement for which there are few words. Some people describe the inner awareness of a creature inside of them, seeming to utter a continuous low wail. Others report being aware of a deep inner darkness which they "see" as a visual background to every waking moment.

I remember speaking with one veteran of the 1st Marine Division's retrograde march out from the Chosin Reservoir in Korea. He cannot talk in detail of those awful days. But this comment is telling in its sparseness, "You know, I have *never* been able to get warm. Even right now, I feel cold," he confided one magnolia scented Richmond afternoon.

At other times the distress occurs at birth or appears to spring fully formed at the bidding of a genetic calendar. As religious counselors, pastors and clinicians we stand here at the very boundary between genius and madness, between the true prophet and the person whom the gods have set out to destroy. The torture and joy of the inner life appears through the word salad of schizophrenese or the complexity of James Joyce's *Ulysses*. Those who seem to bear the burden of retardation have a religious joy many of us may envy. Yet the sheer marginality of their life may make us recoil. To struggle with the deterioration of aging or a life-concluding disease may be enough to completely erase a lifetime of hopefulness. All clinicians are confronted by the sheer unredemptiveness of human suffering in the course of a professional career.

What matters most here is not so much the content of the experience but the profundity of the experience itself.[91] In each instance a human soul is attempting to express what is ineffable, trying to point toward that which is unseeable, longing to connect in some satisfying way with a Being "that than which a Greater cannot exist."[92] A Reality which is at once immanent and transcendent. Yet the core reality which these separate individuals all grope to express is one which, apparently, is utterly debasing. They truly believe they are beyond the reach of the Almighty One. It is as though in some way they have been inducted into a secret fellowship of suffering from which all others have been excluded. Including God.

For such persons the language of defilement seems to evoke the most self-awareness. The cry of abandonment seems to resonate most deeply within their experience. It is the fundamental recognition that one has been in an unholy place, seen or done unholy acts, heard unholy words and crossed the boundary which separates their living soul from what they know is more traditionally spoken human experience. In our religious, clinical rush to soothe every ache and pronounce grace upon every sin, we may be sorely tempted to gloss over a person's report of such primitive feelings. In particular, our modern church music and liturgies soft pedal this element in religious life. In attempting to be non-offensive we may offend what is most Holy in both the person and in the universe. If we do not speak the language of defilement or acknowledge the depth of abandonment to which the human soul can sink, then we have no genuine good news to offer those for whom this has become their primary experience.

Defilement and the Symbolism of Stain

Stains come in various ways but they remind us that something is fundamentally flawed. Whether it is our shirt's visible memory of a hurried cup of coffee or a sidewalk's memory of a murder, stains symbolize an event which was vital. Stains are a snapshot of the past which haunts us in the present. We may joke about the hunting jacket which gets its oil changed every decade whether it needs it or not. But the real jacket is a visual statement in the present of the owner's past activity. While it is a badge of honor among other hunters there are many places where such a visual and vital statement would make people recoil. We do not feel neutral about stains. Stains symbolize our uncleanness. Stains picture our flaws. Stains are not only left *upon* us they are tangible memories of things we have *done upon* the world - our world. Stains symbolize "a 'something' that infects, a dread that anticipates the unleashing of the avenging wrath of the interdiction" for the taboo which the stain symbolizes.[93]

Stains shock us. Several years ago a young woman who described herself as a Performance Artist drew the outline of a body on the sidewalks where a rape had occurred. The public outcry was immediate and intense! Imagine! In *Richmond!* Someone leaving a mark on an *historic* sidewalk! People were much more upset by the "stain" left by her white paint than the human stain left by the rapes. For those of us who lived or worked in the neighborhood, her staining art was a sobering reminder of our shared vulnerability, our impotence and our guilty lack of outrage.

Religious consciousness is filled with the symbolism of stain. One of the most ancient Biblical stories carries the image of a stain or mark left upon Cain. While the function of the mark was to protect him from revenge, its presence functioned as a continual reminder of his homicide.[94] Significantly this story speaks of both the soil and the person bearing a stain as a permanent mark of defilement. One of the dominant images of absolution is that of cleansing a stain, a reality reinforced by our Psalms of penitence such as Psalm 51 and hymnody such as *Love Lifted Me:*

> I was sinking, deep in sin
> Far from the peaceful shore,
> Very deeply stained within,
> Sinking to rise no more,
> But the Master of the Sea
> Heard my despairing cry,
> From the waters lifted me,
> Now safe am I,[95]

Stains upon the heart are more than powerful metaphor. Stains typically have their antecedent in real fluids which are present as an integral part of the defiling action. It can be as fundamental as the discoloration of a woman's birth water which signals major infant distress. Indeed the monthly cycle of menstruation has been, perhaps unfairly but nonetheless realistically, a continuing symbol for feminine weakness. Semen spilled during a rape or molestation, bloody tubercular phlegm, vomit encrusted clothing from alcohol poisoning, bandages upon a wound and our deep dread of blood carrying the AIDS virus are genuine substances which imprint real scars upon both body and soul. Our obsession with soaps and scents for home and self reveals how deeply we desire to avoid being, or at least showing, our stains to one another. We avoid people and places that are stained. They are unholy and profane. Although Ricoeur argues that "defilement was never literally a stain; impurity was never literally filthiness, dirtiness," clinicians may find that inquiry into the exact nature of a person's distress does, indeed, lodge within the memory of a literal stain.[96]

Our secular culture tells stories of unholy stains and longs for rites to cleanse stains no less than our religious communities. The most potent stories are ones which symbolize the utter transformation and damnation of people who have contact with the blood of another. These are the myths of vampires and werewolves. These stories do more than scare small children around campfires. We may walk out of the movie theater's darkness saying, "It deserved the two thumbs up Siskle and Ebert gave it!" But in the darkness of the theater our pulse raced because we were truly fearful. Our hair stood on end and our skin crawled because we recoiled in genuine dread. Our science may tell us such creatures and unholy transformations do not occur. But our unconscious which comes from the dawn of our existence remains unconvinced. We react with revulsion. The impact of such fundamental brokenness upon a life is difficult to gauge. For a majority of persons the dynamics of their stains and the feeling of dread do not incapacitate them. Most of us can wall off or repress such memories. We continue with our lives in what we believe to be a pathway unaffected by such fundamental tragedy. But there are others among us whose flaws are so overwhelming that the barriers of repression and impulse control are overwhelmed. A few of these persons will seek the care of a pastor, the hope embodied in a religious community or the relative sanctuary of a psychiatric facility. Many more will not. We will instead perceive glimpses of their stain upon the pages of our society's daily record. Ricoeur's comment that "primitive dread deserves to be interrogated as our oldest memory" may be fruitful advice for clinicians, whether their orientation is secular or religious.[97]

Defilement and the Saving Sacrifice

Her dreams are always vivid. They have plagued her sleep for years, because their violent and bloody content is so at odds with her serene and fastidious appearance. Sometimes Rose is fleeing in horror from a faceless man who wields a knife. Other times she is in a junk yard watching a man drag a woman into a bedroom. Often she is sheltering a group of children. Her cries often wake her up.

"I fear I am losing my mind," she said. "My life is not this horrible." As our work progressed through the first year of conversation, another image began appearing alongside of the bloody violence: water. Sometimes there was a tile bathroom shower or a nearby river. In other dreams the setting is a seaside cabin or she watches rain wash the grime from a darkened city street through the glass wall of an urban apartment.

Then one day Rose said, "We're not going to get anywhere unless I tell you what really has happened." So in a voice nearly devoid of emotion she recounted being tied up on her wedding night. She has remembered three ministers, so far, who have assaulted her while also telling her she "was helping God's work." She remembered her mother's long-standing frailty, along with the cryptic instructions that she and her husband would "work out an arrangement."

The events behind this woman's dread and stain continued to surface. But like her mother before her, she did not leave her abusive husband. She did not transfer to a job where her boss was not predatory. She had made a decision to endure continued staining and humiliation for the sake of the safety of others. Rose soothes the dread and tames her emerging rage with medication.

Sacrifice is one of the basic ways which we cope with the profound abandonment of such assaults upon our being. Whether it is the parent who interposes themself between a child and danger or, just as likely, a child who decides to offer a portion of their self for family stability, the dynamic element in the event is one of partial self-slaughter. There always comes the heroic moment when a living soul chooses the unknown depths of abandonment in a desperate gamble to forestall the known horror which confronts them. We give medals to soldiers who make such a sacrifice. But many more people make similar offerings of the self and go on living as though nothing has happened. Thus the counselor may live and work for years beside another who is deeply stained by some prior sacrifice of psyche and soma yet be unaware of the events which have so profoundly shaped the person's current life.

There are a number of clinical profiles which have such saving sacrifice at their root. Multiple Personality Disorder, Anorexia and Bulimia come readily to mind. But even where there is not such profound disturbance in the outer life there can be a staining sacrifice. Depression which robs one of hope, anxiety which disrupts one's peace, repetitive unemployment as well as pervasive drug dependence and cyclic infidelity may all have a core memory of a stain whose outline we can see only through repetitive behavior. The clinical description of "personality traits that are inflexible and maladaptive and cause significant functional impairment or subjective distress" begins to approach this area of religious interest.[98] While religious diagnosis lacks the specificity of Schizoid Personality Disorder (301.20) with full-blown differential diagnostic options, the existential dimension of human experience is no less genuine and the language of stain no less descriptive of the person's dilemma.

Conclusion

Religious sensitivity in general and the theological training of pastors specifically equips them to understand the profound connection symbols have upon the human soul. Symbols obtain their numinosity precisely because they participate in the awesome, dread acts to which they point us. Thus the mute anguish of many people is a religious awareness of the ineffableness of the staining acts to which they have been a party. Our spiritual awareness of such connections embody the hope of healing for others, for we may understand more than many that new life and resurrection awaits us. But resurrection comes only after one faces the dread abandonment of an *Old Rugged Cross,* has been touched by the *Balm in Gilead* and has drunk deeply from the Cup of Transformational Suffering. Only the religiously attuned counselor can use the healing story of Jacob's Well, listening there to another thirsty person's confusion and reminding them of the Spirit's living water .[99]

Chapter 8

Feeling Dread

The February sky in Washington, D. C. filled the streets with cold slush. It soaked through my boots, chilling my feet as I walked to the Memorial. "Just a quick stop," I thought. "No sense in not seeing the Vietnam Memorial, since I'm here." But the feeling in the pit of my stomach as I put my foot on the brick pathway told me this would not be a perfunctory nod to one more national shrine. The feeling was not fear, for I was calm and very aware of my surroundings. The feeling was dread, for I knew that I would finally be coming face to face with a place commemorating my own staining. As Thomas Merton notes, this type of dread is a "sense that one had been untrue to one's own inmost truth," a truth I had avoided until then. [100]

It was suddenly warm. At least, I felt warm. Time was different, as though I had an eternity of moments. There was a crush of people there and yet I felt completely solitary.

Then I found the names.

Where mine could also have been.

I was shivering, weeping, laughing and praying all at once. I knelt on the wet earth.

Then there was a soft hand on my shoulder, "It's okay, Marine. You are home and they are at peace."

I never knew whose hand and voice came out of that anonymous crowd. But I knew that in those words my dread had been released.

I have returned to this place several times as a pastor and as a private citizen. The Wall always moves me but the feeling of dread is gone.

In a culture satiated with images of terror and violence the distinc-

71

tion between terror and dread may be a subtle one. The primary dynamic in terror is fright and the impulse to run away. The primary dynamic in dread is awe and the impulse to remain still. Dread is the basic emotional datum of religious experience, where we move through the wind, fire and earthquake to hear ourselves addressed in some fashion by the Still Small Voice.[101]

Dread is also the basic emotional datum of returning to the place and person of our staining. Here we wonder once again at the complex bond between events which both shattered our world and formed it into its present constellation. Dread is what you experience when you come once more to the nexus of creation and destruction. Part of the task of healing may be to journey with someone else who wishes to revisit this stained crossroads in their heart so that they may take another road.

Journey to the Crossroads

He had telephoned me from an Indiana crossroads nearly not on the map. After driving for an hour, his car pulled up in front of the church. "Mind if we walk outside rather than sit in the study?" he asked. "Sure, " I said. "This is the kind of town where everyone knows you're not from *here* anyway. Walking outside is just as private as staying inside."

We spent the Summer taking early evening walks, once or twice a week, as he detailed the hideous outlines of an abusive, crazy family. Father's alcoholism produced fearsome rages from which there was no escape. "Next door" was three miles away. Mother had drawn him early to her bedroom for mutual comfort. His sisters had turned him into a pet. An early photograph of him with his sisters and mother showed everyone wearing dresses and laughing. It gave me the sickening feeling of seeing a family feeding on itself.

"I don't know if Daddy knew about this," he confided. "Mommy called it 'our little secret.' I came to the point where I would run home from the school bus stop and find their clothes. It felt like a game, at first."

Then one day there was a long pause in our conversation. "Can we go back to the church?" he asked. "There's something I want to tell you, but I think doing it in church would be safer, somehow."

So we walked a few moments and came to the country sanctuary's unlocked door. We sat down near the front, on the right. It was quiet except for the blackbirds singing in the soybean field. "O God," he began, "I am sure I'm a girl. Why have You trapped me here, in this man's body?" It was a simple question. Not shouted or sobbed. But it was a powerful query, made potent by the silence into which he uttered it.

Quite apart from the genetic questions involved in such a complex case, transexualism appears to bring together two areas where defilement and stain produce the strongest affective response and greatest cognitive dissonance: murder and sexuality.[102] In a basic way transexualism may be understood as a type of self-murder which expresses the person's profound sense of defilement.

Jerry's story and his primary question is a profoundly human one once the twisted details of his anguish are removed. What helped him give voice to his deepest doubt there on a September afternoon? What are the necessary and sufficient ingredients which a religious counselor may use to assist and sustain another who is journeying to such a mesmerizing crossroads?

The basic skills of counseling are well known. They are attending, paraphrasing, reflection of feeling, probing, counselor self-disclosure, interpretation, summarizing and confrontation. Counselors of various theoretical viewpoints combine these skills in unique but recognizable patterns to assist the persons who come to them for help. There is not a special skill needed to approach the depthful stain of dread within another human being. What is required is a sensitivity to the explicit content, images and themes of sacrificial stains within the life of the person as they unfold their anguish.

Thus walking with Jerry was a way of attending to him in a manner that he felt comfortable. Using phrases such as "you sound embarrassed," or "you sound ashamed," or "I wonder if you feel stained" reflected feelings which, when he confirmed them, drew him toward his basic wound. Asking for clarity, such as "where did your Mother touch you?" or "how early did your sisters dress you up?" is probing. "It sounds as though you were all hungry for tenderness," is interpretation.

The reader may wonder at the intentional use of a diagnostic framework's metaphor (stain) to guide inquiry with someone else. The assumptive model that may therapists adopt appears to be that the therapist is a *tabula rasa* onto which the client projects their feelings without intrusion by the therapist. This is a nice model. It is an unrealistic model, whose lived reality is much different. All diagnostic models use a framework to discern the level of pain and the scope of damage in another person. Whether we ask "how long have you felt discouraged about your future?" or "how long have you felt deeply stained?" we are conducting responsible diagnosis so that we can adequately name the pain and guide the care of the person.

The skill of attending is particularly important with someone who is damaged at this existential or genetic level. In order for the person to feel safe enough to disclose this layer of the soul, they must be very certain of the counselor's unwavering presence with them. This comes from the basic dread which this type of trauma implants within the heart: that the Other will "kill" or at least recoil in horror once the dreadful stain is revealed.[103]

The ability to attend deeply to another's existential discomfort is the key counselor attribute for reaching this level of another's stain. This is empathy. Although much research indicates that a person will become attached most easily with someone with whom they perceive the closest affinity, the perception which apparently counts the most is this attentional affinity on the part of the care provider. The pastor's race, gender, sexual orientation may help in the initial encounter. But these surface descriptors will not sustain her if she lacks a more fundamental ability to attend to these depths. In the initial portion of this journey, the skills of attending, reflection of feeling, paraphrasing and sometimes probing for information aids the most directly to the client's experience of our attention. Counselor self-disclosure, interpretation and confrontation should be used very sparingly, if at all. Summarizing, such as "so what you're really saying is. . . ." especially when followed by an empathic comment such as "that must have felt. . . ." or "I wonder how it feels to you to hear this summary?" can reinforce the reality of the counselor's abiding presence with the suffering person.

Standing At The Crossroads

"How do you know when a person is revisiting the place or memory of their staining?" is a typical query from supervisees.

"Its a bit like crossing into Laos from Vietnam," I reply. "There aren't any road signs which say *Welcome to Laos!* but everything begins to feel much more serious. The air is alive with dread." This is not a flippant answer. It is an attempt to realistically describe an experience which is at the boundary of human language. It is also an effort to encourage counselors of all types, whether religious or secular, to develop their *third ear* to actually *hear* this quality in the human voice. Managed care plans won't give you time to listen for it and HMO's won't have a space for it on their treatment plans. But without this skill much of our counseling is going to read like a neighborhood coffee klatch. Since pastors especially are people who work at the boundary of language, of what is speakable, we should not be too uncomfortable with acquiring such a set of ears.

Yet there are some indicators we are approaching this doorway in the soul. A person's breath will usually be more shallow. Although they may have been restless up to this point, they will usually become physically still. Their voice will drop in volume but not in clarity. They may cough or clear their throat. The caregiver likewise may feel as though there is a great weight pushing them back into their chair. They may find themselves mesmerized by the person's eyes or face. The counselor may even feel suddenly groggily, a not altogether unusual response of the human to holy ground.[104]

One cannot predict what the person may do at this point in the journey. It may be helpful to ask, softly, "It there something you need to say or do?" But mostly what seems to be efficacious is the counselor's own stabilizing, empathic and silent presence.[105] Some people may regress quite far, by screaming loudly, curling up in a ball, pounding a soft pillow, cursing or speaking in tongues. Others may report *ex post facto* that they have heard a voice giving them instructions or peaceful reassurance. The client may see a vision. Whether *we* understand these encounters to be with the Collective Unconscious, the Ground of Being or God Almighty, the *person* invariably recounts such events as ones in which they are touched by a Holy Presence.

One of the most powerful of such encounters I can recall was with a refugee from Cambodia. He had come to America and done very well. But after everyone from his family was safely here, the depression and nightmares started. It was as though all the horror of those killing fields had been finally let loose within his sleep. In our halting con-

versation I finally asked him if there was someone, more than any
other one, whose torment he could not shake.

There came a deep stillness. He nodded," Yes." I then invited him
to picture this one person being in the room with us. The look in his
eyes over the next few moments went from sadness to fear to dread
and then, finally, to a hard fury.

At this point I asked him, "Do you need to say anything to this
man?"

"Yes, but cannot say only in Khmer," was his reply."

"Then say in Khmer," I said.

What followed was about five minutes of Khmer pouring out of his
heart. I could not translate what he was saying. But I *knew* what he
was saying. His experience of lament and confrontation at the crossroads of his stain is a universal experience. The hair on the back of
my neck was standing on end. His eyes were watering but his hands
were absolutely still. For those few minutes we were in Cambodia at
some unnamed but well-remembered place of his suffering.

We may also stand at such a crossroads with someone who is much
less lucid. I remember an incident in the locked ward of a nursing
home which received patients from within a state mental health system. These persons' abilities to function were minimal, since they required almost total care. One man would lay in bed, pounding upon
his chest with one unrestrained hand while shouting at the top of his
lungs. He did this for roughly ten hours a day. Feeding him, chang-
ing his diaper and making up his bed was more than a moderate challenge for the staff.

But one day when I entered the room to feed him, I remember praying quietly, "O Lord, help me see this man as You see him." As I
walked toward his bed, he turned to me with his screaming, wild-eyed
pounding. His appearance, to my perception, seemed to grow softer.

I was not totally aware that his shouting diminished to the point of
silence until his breakfast was done and I turned around to see other
staff members standing at the door watching. It was absolutely still.

"What did you do?" the head nurse asked. Since I was as dumb-
founded as she was, I couldn't really give her an answer. Yet on the
following days of my work there, this man would become still when I
entered his room with an intentional presence. Clearly we were visiting some place within his being, a place where words and touch were
not too useful. When I have shared this vignette with others who work

in such environs, they report similar periodic encounters with profoundly disturbed persons. Most frequently it is the aides, janitors and sometimes the chaplains who have such experiences. I am not suggesting that such an intentioned effort always, or even frequently produces such an encounter. All I am suggesting is that we need a way of speaking about such exchanges within our diagnostic model. We need a way of honoring this stillness, a way of describing such quiet that values the inherent worth of persons and does not hear this quiet as simply the cessation of an overactive limbic system or merely an aspect of counter-transference. We must again allow the clinical time and space wherein "this deep dread and night must then be seen for what it is: not as punishment, but as purification and as grace."[106]

Conclusion: Choosing Another Road

For the man just mentioned, his new road was one which contained periods of stillness. For Jerry his new road was the eventual ability to return to his psychologist and more fairly evaluate his desire for sex reassignment surgery. For persons of more average sensibility, such a crossroads often involves a new vocational choice. In some instances the individual may change their name. A move to a new part of the city or country is not out of the question.

For the religious counselor who walks with someone to the point of vocational change, there are both secular and spiritual resources. Typically within the religious community we speak of this in the language of discernment or spiritual direction. The strength of these approaches is their ability to allow the deeper wells of the unconscious to fully come forward. They emphasize the creative aspect of the person's newly forming self-identity.

One handicap for pastors and religious counselors is that we lack specific information about the breadth of vocational opportunity. Thus a pastor who is providing care for someone who reaches this decision point may be wise to suggest a visit to a vocational resource center at a local high school or university. Use of the *Strong Interest Inventory* or the *16PF Career Development Profile* can be useful adjuncts for both secular and religious counselors. The current flux within the American employment picture, especially within the more technical fields, makes it nearly impossible for any counselor or pastor to keep up with the breadth of vocational and career options.

The religious community has historically announced that a person's work is a fundamental expression of their devotion to God. We owe it to those who seek our counsel to direct them in a way in which they will be able to utilize their abilities to the utmost. To simply suggest that the person check out the want ads or ask their current employer for a raise minimizes the depth of change they have embarked upon. Another handicap is the inherent ineffability of the experience. Like all depthful religious experiences, one cannot always say with certainty either what has taken place or what the outcome of the event will be. As long as the official pastoral care movement remains primarily driven by a mental health model, clinicians may have difficulty find-- ing language to describe the client's experience. How does a religious clinician describe such events as these to an insurance company's case manager? Prognosis about the "length of treatment" is a category which may not be merely tentative but quite improper to apply to this type of counseling. We may have to put the welfare of the person above the strictures for third-part reimbursement. We may have to state the pastor's distinctive contribution to the healing journey in spite of an inherent inability to specify what the outcome may be or when it will arrive.

In a recent article in the *Journal of Pastoral Care,* Dr. Mary Louise Bringle illustrates both the evocative power of "images to dwell in, to amplify and elaborate as we try to understand the many threads of this life-weaving which we variously label depression or despair or the dark night of the soul." She suggests images "of braided strands, colored dye and salt and the alchemists' and mystics' black sun.[107]" These images bring with them a rich history that certainly speaks powerfully to the inner experience of troubled persons. But few secular clinicians are familiar with the history in these metaphors. Although she wants to "weave" this schema into "an Axis VI for the dimension of *Spirituality,*" she offers no guidance in doing so that would be comprehensible to either a secular clinician or a case manager.[108]

This may signal the poverty of contemporary mental health practice. It does indicate the need for additional depthful dialog between religious and secular clinicians so that we benefit from one another's diagnostic language in a way that assists our clients.

Chapter 9

Rediscovering Joy

"You would hardly recognize Angie now," said her mother. Angie had been referred to a child specialist at a regional medical center after traditional play therapy and initial testing had failed to dislodge her pervasive pattern of failure and defiance. A complete physical and neurological exam had disclosed a hearing loss and her need for glasses. Involvement in group therapy and structured homework guidelines helped her express herself in less defiant ways. She also learned desperately needed study skills.

"Thank God for Dr. Smith," her mother said. "I was beginning to despair of Angie ever getting any help. She's a different person!"

"Sounds like you're a bit different too," the therapist commented over the telephone. "You sound positively joyful."

"Yes! Even though there are difficult days, they are nothing like what we had," she replied. "But more important, I do *enjoy* her again. I feel as though I've gotten back the daughter who was lost. I even have begun to believe that I can be a good mother."

Joy is precisely this fundamental sense of universal delight, tinged with a perception of well-being. Joy is a posture of gratitude which persists in spite of current disappointment or irritation. Joy, or at least its cousins of happiness and delight, seem to be something we all want. But joy is one of the most elusive states of being. Joy is shy. She comes to us only after we have endured the hurricane, survived as a captive or cleared away the mountain trail's underbrush. Announcing that we have "found the son who was lost"[109] inviting others to "come and meet the man who told me everything I ever did"[110] or singing along with Handel's *Messiah* all point toward the discovery of joy.

For some people the process of religious care may never touch this layer of renewal. Yet there are persons who come for help precisely because they have grown tired of their guilt, alienation and dread. They come longing to be touched by a Gracious God. They come in the hope that this One who dwells in ineffable light will glow within their hearts and shield them from drought or famine. Because diagnosis is not simply about naming the pain but also about guiding the care / cure, pastors and clinicians need to have some idea of how to guide another soul toward this ultimate surprise.

A Visitation of Butterflies and Night Rainbows

It seemed that everyone else in the county had seen her husband's pickup truck outside of the woman's house. Except her. "They must have all been laughing at me," she said one biting March day. In April she struggled valiantly through the sale of the farm, watching strangers bid on family land. But May came and there was no place to plant a garden. There would be no beans to stuff into thick Mason jars. No tomatoes would ripen on her window. She stopped attending church. Her phone rang, unanswered.

Then when the winter wheat was being harvested and the sweaty crews were plowing for soybeans right behind the combines, she appeared at my door. Her face was glowing! She sat in my study for awhile, eyes bright and silent. "I just had God visit me," she said. "I hope you don't think I am crazy. I went into the wood lot, even though we don't own it anymore. I just drove there anyway," she said a bit self-consciously. "I just started weeping and I thought about running a hose into the car from the exhaust. The window was open. And in through the window came a butterfly! It sat right on the steering wheel and looked at me! Pastor, I know this sounds crazy, but it *looked* at me. A wave of peace came over me which I cannot describe. But I knew, *I know!* that I am going to be all right. The butterfly wasn't God, I guess, but it felt like it came right from God as a messenger of hope."

In the days and months ahead, Ruth would refer back to this butterfly. She drew a painting of it. She brought a butterfly sun catcher to hang in her kitchen window. She began to tell others who were also on suicide's brink about the butterfly. "Call me if you need to talk," she would say. While not every story has such a joyful resolution, we must not build our religious care solely around the failures in care. There are times, probably more often than we know about where the Divine Spirit breaks through in answer to a person's heartfelt cry.[111]. We know the marks of such experiences very well, except when religious counselors put on their *clinical* orientation. My experience as a supervisor is that often the religious counselor suddenly become skeptical about their religious good news whenever they perceive they must become *clinical*. This lack of professional and personal integration does not bode well for patient care. This historic struggle to integrate profound religious experience within the clinical setting continues into our most contemporary treatments on this subject.[112]

Profound religious experiences have three defining aspects. First, these experiences come to us in their own time and not upon our demand. Second, encounters with the Spirit do contain an element of awe. We are usually reassured in the moment of a theophany with the traditional *Fear not!* or a subjective awareness that we have nothing to dread. Third, these encounters demand something of us, usually that we undertake a new, difficult or self-giving task.[113]

Since these experiences come unbidden, is there anything for the clinician or pastor to do? Yes! We can set a context of expectation which is worshipful and does not create false hope or maudlin sentimentality. For the community religious leader, the prayers and teachings you offer can witness to a God whose presence is both powerfully transcendent yet gently near at hand. There can be a willingness to use new names for God which exult in majesty and affirm a posture of divine attentiveness. In our conversations with others, as clinicians and religious leaders, we can listen with an attentiveness that communicates by implication the attention of the One Who Visits in the Storm. Here is an example of such a prayer:

> Holy Lord of Unquenchable Light: You come
> to us in the very breath of the stars! Whether in
> the glory of an unblemished dawn or the majesty of a
> winter's crystal night, Thy wonder seeps into the roots of
> our heart! We do not understand such wonder, but we feel
> You with each moment. We cannot express these mysteries,
> but our eyes glow with joyful tears. You beckon us
> through darkness to join Thee in light; You invite us in the
> midst of suffering to be agents of Thy healing.

O Most Holy One, we lift up to You the needs of many. Some
have their faces sealed deep within our souls. Some have left
their touch upon our weathered flesh. Some we cannot name
except in silence. But You hear beyond our words!
Encourage them with the rainbow which glimmers even in
the night! Amen![114]

We can also be the one who receives another's good news. Murphy's
Third Law is "If it's stupid but works, it isn't stupid." This means we
must receive the person's report of religious experience with respect
and attention. The Divine Spirit's way of approaching someone may
not suit our predilections. God may, indeed, ask them to do something
a religious professional would never think of doing. The Wonder's
breath may sweep across another in a way which we feel is not theologically correct, especially if we have confused theology and clinical
health with a scientific world view.[115]

But religious counselors, no less than secular ones, must remember
that God's active self-disclosure must define theology. Not the other
way around. I suspect the reason clergy do not hear as many stories
like Ruth's as actually exist is that the average parishioner fears we
will judge their experience as either inadequate or crazy. They may
have heard enough in the religious and secular media from clergy who
explain away the miraculous to doubt *our* faith. They may have even
gotten this perception from our own public remarks.

In short, there are two things religious professionals can do for those
who seek our care. Foremost we must cultivate our own awareness of
the Holy. Second we can talk about our experience of the Holy. My
hunch is that if we are comfortable with the Holy, those who seek our
counsel may also become able to discover the presence of the One Who
Births the Stars pulsing in their own darkness. Counter-transference
works for more than just recognizing the parallel family histories between pastor / counselor and parishioner / client.[116]

Touching the Warmth of Another

"Is there anything *else* I can do to rid myself of these awful dreams,"
Rose asked one day? "I feel like there is something missing." So she
and her therapist agreed upon a time of drawing with watercolors. A
few weeks later she ended her counseling session with the terse an-

nouncement, "I've started drawing." It would be several weeks before
she brought the completed drawings to her therapist.

"Giving them to you is more frightening than trying to tell you what
they look like," she said. "But I sure can't leave them at home. I don't
want to carry them with me." Her drawings were filled with the crude
but accurate imagery of remembered trauma. Large brush strokes
communicated the power and terror she continued to feel about these
slowly emerging memories. As we continued exploring these painful
offerings, the following exchange often took place:

> Rose: "I still feel as though there is
>   something I should be telling you.
>   But it just doesn't want to come out."
>
> Pastor: "You really want to be relieved of
>   these burdens. Nothing in your past
>   experience prepares you to trust a
>   man. These memories will emerge
>   when they, and you, are ready."

Here we have the desperate longing for the healing touch of another
human being. She waits for the birth of joy in her heart. Too often at
this junction the provider of care succumbs to the temptation for magic
or exhortation. Certainly a well-directed, heartfelt intercessory prayer
or, a *sotte voce* affirmation of one's trustworthiness would speed this
process along. Yet if consistent warmth and empathy are the human
dynamics which lead to healing joy, then the effort to wrest joy from
its hiding place is exactly the *wrong* move to make here.

Rose has felt warmth and power invade her all of her life. She may
be healed only when warmth and power become something, or someone, which she can choose to discover. Thus the healing task is for the
care provider to remain steadfast in communicating empathy while
also retaining the clinical distance necessary which allows the person
to move. It is the Herculean effort required of the person to move *toward* warmth, and not the assertive activity of the counselor, which
allows depthful, life-transforming joy to be born in another's heart.[117]

This type of conversation is quite distinct from typical religious or
pastoral care. Basic pastoral care is rooted in the pastoral privilege to
bless and visit without invitation. It has proactive and evangelistic an-

tecedents in our religious traditions from all sacred writings as well as
our natural inclination to bring mercy to those who are suffering. Yet
walking with another person at this depth requires that the religious
clinician draw upon a different spiritual tradition.

The tradition of Isaiah's Suffering Servant can be instructive to both
secular and religious clinician. The Suffering Servant / Wounded
Healer is a cross-cultural model, a notation by Jung and cited by others
that "the fundamental archetype of all life is wound and healing."[118]
It is this Servant who knows enough to wait in calmness for greatness,
peace and joy to emerge.[119] It is not enough for the religious counselor to quote these verses to a suffering person. For the words to have
healing efficacy we, the counselor, must be willing to wait with the
person. The simple fact is that with Ruth neither she nor her therapist
knew precisely where these drawings might lead. The knew only that
healing was a hoped-for destination.

Thus while strong anguish certainly lay ahead, the counselor's steady
pace was a witness to the non-abandoning warmth of God. Alongside
the one who is groping in confusion and pain, there was One, symbolized by the religious care provider, Who has not fled or come down
hard in force. For persons whose history predisposes them to hear
only blame and condemnation, a pastor's empathy can melt the rigidity
of judgment. For persons whose life experience equips them to con-
fuse joy with beer commercial exuberance, a clinician's straightfor-
ward affirmation can warm their heart in a new and surprising fashion.

Although the experience of joy still lies ahead for Rose, it is now
current experience for Gary. This began in one interview in which he
both lamented his father's inability to be warm toward him during
childhood and then the announcement, "But, Hell, that was nearly 50
years ago. What good is it to deal with all this now?"

"You are a person of value," the counselor replied while looking directly into his eyes.

Gary's eyes glazed as he said, "Holy Christ! I feel like you've just
shot me! Right here in the chest! It hurts. . . . .and I like it! Why did
it take so long to get to this place?"

"You are worth waiting for," was the counselor's reply into Gary's
tear-laced silence. They had walked together for nearly two years.

Conclusion: Celebrating the surprise of life

"I was scared to death when I drove into the country to that little white church," he said over spaghetti and garlic bread. He was remembering a gathering of combat veterans around the altar to tell the stories of battles and of their return to civilian life. "How was I to know that sitting at the communion table and talking with others about what happened in combat would change my life. What a surprise! I hadn't been in any church for nearly twenty years."

There was a pause as he dabbed at the scarlet sauce with his shard of bread.

"You can be that I go there now," he added quietly.

A feeling of profound gratitude can accompany the resolution of existential stain and the birth of joy. The person may feel the strong inclination to do something new or be with people who celebrate new birth. Clergy may have adults come to them with stories of profound transformation who conclude with a request for a "rebaptism." Certainly a number of mid-life vocational changes come about in an effort to express this joy in a redirected fashion. Such changes in direction or requests for a religious rite to signal significant change are not "mid-life crises." They mark the *resolution* of such a crisis.

Psychotherapy is by its very nature extremely private. Thus after the termination session there is nearly always a permanent parting of the ways. One shuts the door, hopefully with some degree of finality, on a troubling part of the psyche.

But pastoral care and life in a religious community is different. While one would not dredge up the details of confessional care into public worship, most religious traditions have a range of public rites available which may help the individual, couple or family symbolize their gratitude. The religious leader can legitimately offer such rites of recognition to an individual. The religious leader can also ethically offer to the recovering person membership in a community of historic joy whereas the secular therapist may only wish the person well as they continue their life.

The public practice of giving a testimony within the evangelical tradition is one time honored practice. So is the practice of reaffirming marital vows. There are other ways someone can celebrate their emergence from the Pit and share their joy with a community of faith. Writing a new hymn, performing instrumental or vocal music, agreeing to serve in an outreach ministry or simply practicing the gift of hospitality can be ways of an individual doing something new and expressing their gratitude. Can such actions be abused, by either the unreconstructed narcissist or the exploitative pastor? Of course. But these caveats should not preclude the judicious use of grateful people in the ongoing public life of the community which sponsors the provider of religious care.

The essence of joyful public worship is the *experience* of joy. An exegetical sermon on the linguistic roots of "joy" may inform the community but the robust singing of joyful hymns will infuse people with joy. One need not focus entirely on up-tempo music or vapid lyrics to assist peoples' worshipful and joyful encounter with God. The author's somewhat limited exposure to African American congregations, where the music may last upwards of an hour before the bulk of the liturgy, suggests that joy comes from such a communal encounter even when all of the music is not "happy."

The religious caregiver must not forget that they represent a community which, at its healthiest, exhibits the deepest longing of the human soul. Forgiveness proclaimed in the face of ethical and emotional guilt. Reconciliation embodied upon ground torn apart by conflict. Peace negotiated between a rebellious people and a righteous God. Love demonstrated in the midst of hatred and misunderstanding. Joy celebrated as an antidote to the sting of despair. It is primarily within the religious community, with its millennia-spanning tradition of celebrating the redemptive presence of God, where one can find both the language of joy and the affirmation of God as the Ultimate Surprise - The One Beside Us All Along. In summarizing his work both as a chaplain and patient at Worcester State Hospital, Anton Boisen on the influence of the church:

> From the therapeutic standpoint the church at its best is a group of imperfect persons united on the basis of an ideal which they are seeking to realize in their own lives and in the social order. Of all institutions the church, despite its weaknesses and shortcomings, is the one in which men meet on their highest levels, where they confess their weaknesses and sins with the assurance of social understanding and support and yet without any lowering of standards.[120]

When such moments happen in a religious community or when a religious community matures to the point where such experiences become the norm, then there is truly cause for joy.

Summary

Chapter 10

Diagnosis, Piety and Theology

Religious diagnosis at its best is a complete seeing through of all parties in the caregiving situation. Diagnosis is certainly a naming of the distress which brings the person into care. Yet the practice of diagnosis is more than an expression of clinical acumen. Religious diagnosis points toward the piety and theology of both parties. The secular clinician will necessarily seek to differentiate between Dysthymic Depression and Major Depression without Psychotic Features based upon certain quantifiable criteria. The religious clinician must ultimately rely upon moral discernment, relational perspicuity and spiritual maturity to effect a complete understanding of another's condition.

These are areas of qualitative skill, where people of good will may genuinely differ if the task is to arrive at a numerically precise diagnosis. But if the task of diagnosis is to guide the counselor within a piety and theology upon a pathway which leads to a complete seeing through of the hurting person, then religious caregivers can use this multi-axial system with confidence. The system presented here is also a reminder to the wider community of care providers that there is much about the human person which still remains a mystery and this "sense of the mysteriousness of things has traditionally been one of the mainsprings of the religious as well as of the scientific (psychiatric) impulse."[121] This system is an attempt to assist the clinician in speaking about religious reality clearly. This naturally leaves unsaid the Ultimate Mystery which surrounds us even if we cannot name it, per the dictum "what can be said at all can be said clearly, and what we cannot talk about we must pass over in silence."[122] Or as another writer opined, "Surely I spoke of things I did not understand, things too wonderful for me to know."[123]

A major portion of the truly religious crises which bring people into counseling appear to turn on matters of piety rather than theology. The guilt, depression, anxiety, rage and terror which haunts a number of people seems to come more from a transgression of some religious practice rather than the sudden decision to renounce a cherished theological tenant. The popular notion of pervasive "Catholic guilt," the tragi-comic figure of the "Jewish Mother," or the picture of John Calvin's straight backed chair at Geneva all highlight the ways our pieties wound us.

Thus a religious care provider must routinely discern if the person's distress comes from misapplied piety or a deeply held but denaturing theology. This is not an easy task, since often we counsel people within our own religious tradition. It is difficult to see the plank in our own eye. It is also difficult to discern the planks within our tradition's piety and theology. It may be the wisest course to learn which pietistic issues and theological themes evoke counter-transference within us and refer persons with these concerns to others, much as we would with any other clinical dynamic. Even if it means they may leave the fellowship of our particular faith. We cannot be all things to all people as clinicians nor can our particular theology provide a safe haven for every person, as much as this may threaten us and our heritage to acknowledge this as true.

The sheer diversity of religious need among people called upon by hospital chaplains in one study is striking. Out of 50 cancer patients interviewed, 13 mentioned religion spontaneously and a total of 32 patients "had concerns involving religious issues." These concerns ranged from "recent loss of religious support" and "pressure to adopt[124] a different religious position" to "conflict between religious views and view of the illness" and "preoccupation with the meaning of life and illness."[125] These are concerns which bear directly on patient well-being and even their recovery. Yet there is hardly a way to evaluate and normalize these concerns, let alone converse about them meaningfully among the various caregivers upon whose ministrations the patient's care depends. John Foskett's observation that "religious concerns rarely appears in the pages of psychiatry's text books."[126] and his observation about chaplains in mental health environments, "their contributions always seem marginal to the main purpose of psychiatric hospitals" is hardly comforting for the religiously sensitive patient.[127]

Naturally the above assumes that a client has connection with an identifiable religious tradition. In contemporary America this is increasingly not the case; rather, we see people whose alienation is more fundamental. We are alienated from what earlier centuries called "soul." Religious counselors may be the ones most comfortable with this language and the techniques of helping a person rediscover the "depth, value, relatedness, heart and personal substance which truly defines them."[128] Although Thomas Moore and other contemporary writers quickly add that by "soul" they "do not use the word here as an object of religious belief or as something to do with immortality," their attempt to use this language without explicit reference to objects of religious belief may disclose part of the problem.[129] Rediscovery of explicit religious belief, and even submission to such discipline, may be the avenue to healing for a person. Religious rites, the piety they express and the theology which undergirds them may be more helpful to the soul than our postmodern sophistication is initially willing to grant.

What a religious clinician hears as ethical, relational or existential distress will be affected by their religious practice (piety) and theoretical understanding (theology). As an example, just imagine consulting the Reverend Billy Graham, Bishop James Spong and the Reverend Robert Schuller for a diagnosis and treatment plan on any one of your cases. Nevertheless, each of these individuals would take seriously the importance of connection with a community of faith for the care and cure of a person to be efficacious. As a way of illustrating this multiaxial system at work, and interfacing with your religious understanding, please consider the following case.

The Case of the Discarded Lover

Her tears were visible even in the waiting room. Her sigh after sitting down betrayed her heavy heart as she began to sob. In the broadest outlines of her pain, she is one more casualty of an office romance gone sour. But pain is never generic. This loss appeared to be the final blow. A brochure from a nearby pastoral counseling agency, left in her church's social hall, had guided her to a counselor's office.

An early first marriage to a man who turned out to be actively psychotic had started her on this road to "Hell's Doorway" as she called the place inside where she now lived. A child's drug use and psychosis had followed, casting her in the role of being permanent caretaker. Her work became her one respite. She advanced rapidly. This allowed her to keep a sense of purpose and value through her first divorce. Her second husband, while devoted, was the opposite of her first husband. Rigid and demanding, the disorganized behavior of her psychotic adolescent proved to be too much for him. He insisted the child be banished from the house. The death of her father, "I was his favorite one," seemed to be the final loss which positioned her to someone's caring advances.

They had begun working together. He applauded her skill and intelligence. She admired his competence. She responded eagerly to the extra work. Promotions soon followed. Although his first advance to her was shocking, she said, "I realized I enjoyed him. Nobody else has ever made me feel this alive! I would have continued forever. But its over now, and he feels so cold to me. He treats me like I don't even exist. On top of this, I left the department where I was happy for another department, at his suggestions. He said it would help my career. Now I see that he was just positioning me so he could drop me."

"I hurt all over inside," she concluded. "I want to stop crying but I can't. And I want to know why I don't feel guilty. I committed a sin. I chose him! But I don't feel guilty. For once in my life I had felt really alive. Now I feel really dead inside. I just don't have anymore hope."

Although she denies feeling affective guilt, she brings pain from a clear violation of her own ethical code. Her ethical sensitivity was expressed in the fear of being caught. She feared the punishment of a divorce and the loss of her profession if the affair was discovered. Her concern that the counselor's records might be accessible to her husband signaled this fear even though she projected the fear onto her husband. "I wouldn't want to hurt him," she said often. She used a debit card to pay her bill each time. She didn't want any statements sent to her home or office. All of these signals were indicators that she felt guilt and knew that she had crossed a conventional moral boundary. She returned to this theme of guilt repeatedly, finally naming her sense of sin by saying, "I am an adulteress. I just don't feel guilty."

Using this multi-axial system, the clinician would note her ethical dilemmas on **Axis I.** The clinician could note the ethical tension between her highly developed concern for not harming either her husband or the other man yet her pattern of engaging in behavior which placed two careers and two marriages at substantial risk. She has done great self-harm through things which, if exposed, would bring pain to a variety of people. Thus while she denies feeling guilty, the clinician could focus some of the interventions around the fear of punishment which she exhibits. "For someone who doesn't seem to feel guilty, you spend a great deal of time worrying about getting caught and punished," could be one intervention.

While her ethical boundaries appear to be quite well developed, around this particular set of circumstances she appears to be operating at a very primitive level. Her professionalism and personal scrupulosity appear to place her overall moral development at the level of Convention.[130] Regarding the events of her affair, she seems to have acted at the most basic level of self interest, with the emerging fear of punishment through exposure just surfacing. Thus some of her pain is not yet true guilt but is, instead, the anguish one feels when growing from a basic level of moral awareness to a more advanced level. This is an important distinction for the care provider. As the client works through the layers of affective grief around her loss, she may begin to feel true guilt. When she begins to see the extent of damage to herself and her current marriage which this affair has done, her guilt and sense of impending punishment may be crippling.

She certainly reports feeling punished by the "other man." At the early stage of counseling the feeling of punishment was focused in an extroverted fashion, "I wonder if he dropped me for someone else." His ability to walk by her office door "without so much as a smile" also felt punishing to her. She wondered what she could have possibly *done* to this man, or what could have happened to him to turn him into someone who became cold and uncaring toward her.

The more theological depths of feeling punished would surface only when she would review the wider course of her losses. Then she would use words like "bruised all over," "shaken around inside," and "shattered" to describe the cumulative impact of these losses. All of these feelings and the events which gave rise to them could be noted and explored on **Axis I - Ethical Concerns.**

Naturally the dynamics of any extramarital affair place the caregiver and person squarely within the domain of betrayed covenants addressed on **Axis II.** This wonderful "other man" whom she had counted upon to save her from an unsatisfying marriage had failed to deliver on his promise. Where there had been surprising flowers and intimate after-work dinners which renewed her sense of purpose, now there was only icy silence and her empty lunch box. She had focused a substantial portion of her inner attentiveness and social activity around their mutual desires. "How could he do this to me?" the query of many people who are betrayed by an object of their affection, became one of her routine questions. She felt scorned. As therapy proceeded her fury toward this man would intensify.

At first she sought to understand this man's motivation. Much like any other devoted follower, she sought to explain his new behavior by fitting it into a wider framework. If successful, this would enable her to avoid the terror of her abandonment and the rage of her betrayal. By understanding her abandoning lover she would be able to place him back upon the pedestal in her heart. The theology of Venus, that love is fickle but nonetheless worthy of utter devotion, could thus remain intact. Her lover, although tarnished, could remain in her pantheon of gods.

Cognitive interventions highlighting her overly involved attention, such as "you certainly spend allot of energy trying to figure out someone who has hurt you," were an important step in providing her a safe spot from which to begin feeling her rage. Initially her rage surfaced through her depression. The strength of her depression revealed how much rage she wished to avoid. Yet there was also the danger of suicide if she did not express this rage affectively. Allowing the rage to fester inside of her was deadly. Thus affective interventions which drew her attention toward her anger, and away from obsessing about his feelings or motives, played a crucial step in her early treatment. During the middle stage of religious conversation, where she would revisit the numerous prior sanctuaries that were now reminders of her betrayal, empathic comments would help her stay the course of facing and expressing the very pit of this bitter reversal.

Her experience of betrayal went well beyond the abandonment of this most recent man. Three other males in her life had turned out to be "other than expected." Her current husband had not truly rescued her from the horrors of a failed first marriage or performed as a redeeming father to her troubled son. Her son had been utterly disappointing in his development and continued to wound her with bizarre behavior. Her first husband's mental disorders had likewise been overwhelming. They had served early notice to her that life would not always be what it initially seemed to be or what she would hope it to be.

But there were two more fundamental covenants which had been broken in her life. They formed the base of her rage and seemed to terrify her the most deeply. Whether she and the caregiver would ever finally approach her rage toward the father who had left her by death or the God who placed her in a world where people go psychotic would only emerge in the later stages of therapy. The clinician would need to be aware of these deepest betrayals and alert to them when they began to surface. But to approach them prior to resolving her more immediate feelings related to the affair's termination would be premature. Indeed, resolution of some of the rage related to the "other man" would provide some of the emotional skills necessary for addressing these more fundamental betrayals. Resolving them first would also build therapeutic trust from which these more basic covenants could then be examined.

At the beginning of care the religious caregiver could only surmise a concern which might surface on **Axis III.** She did not present any of the affective signals for dread or use language indicating that she suffered from such a basic disruptions of the self. But there is the issue of her own first child. The diagnostic picture here lacks the clarity of the other two Axes. The differentiating task would be to discern how fully she believed her child's psychosis stemmed from her genetic endowment or if she viewed his brokenness as primarily a condition learned through years of living within an affectively unstable household.

It appeared to the clinician at the beginning of their work together that although she had a theme of defilement on **Axis III,** the defilement seemed to be focused on the child. If long-term care developed with her, then attending and exploring this area would doubtless be necessary. But it appeared that the primary focus of care would be on the concerns of **Axis II:** idolatry and betrayal. These themes, with their attendant feelings of terror and rage would provide ample material for therapeutic conversation.

Naming the Pain and Guiding the Care

Organizing this material into a multi-axial diagnostic format could look like this:

Axis I	*Treatment Considerations*
Ethical Guilt	Ethical development appears focused on conventional concerns.
-	Fears exposure of affair.
-	Feels punished by other man for some yet-unknown failure.
-	Has concerns regarding confidentiality.
-	May have developing legal concerns of sexual harassment.

Axis II	*Treatment Considerations*
Covenantal Betrayal	Religious affiliation Episcopalian but attends Roman Catholic worship.
-	Feels betrayed by lover.
-	Self-description as "adulterer."
-	Multiple betrayals or disruptions of primary covenants - current lover, current husband's failure of care, grown child's chronic psychosis, adoring father's death,
-	God's failure to provide safe and predictable world.

- Feels rage toward
  former lover, exhibited
  primarily as depression.

Axis III Treatment Considerations

Existential Defilement   Primary diagnosis
deferred to Axis II.

- May feel stained as
  result of son's
  chronic psychosis and
  betrayals.
- May attempt suicide
  as symbolic self-
  sacrifice to preserve
  status-quo and resolve
  despair.

A treatment plan for her would have to address short-term and long-term goals. A treatment plan would include affective and cognitive counseling strategies for both areas. A religiously oriented treatment plan would also address strategies for assisting her in resolving her basic sense of covenantal betrayal. The specific modes of care and the way in which the counselor emphasized them will say as much about the clinician's piety and theology as they will disclose about the woman's pain and suffering.

Treatment planning must also take into account the resources in a person's life. This is especially crucial in short-term care, since the person will rely heavily on these resources. Attention to a person's practices, piety and commitments, such as membership in a stable community of faith, will be important. Such a community can provide a web of depthful relationships that extend well beyond the more formal arrangements of clinical therapeutic care.

If religious counselors, especially pastors, truly believe that lay people should be given tasks of ministry, then we must affirm others as sources of wisdom and empathy in the wider mission of the care of souls. Other routine religious activities, including prayer and meditation, devotional reading, and worship attendance can assume a heightened importance during the times of struggle. Religious sacraments such as the Eucharist and, within the Roman Catholic and Reformed traditions, confession and absolution, can also be significant contributors to a person's overall recovery of well being.

A helpful strategy in treatment planning is to ask the person to identify their own religious resources. Inquiry about such resources' current efficacy can be a part of the gentle therapeutic probing done early in the intake process. Here too the clinician's own piety and theology will surface, for the wounded person may have items which are resources to them which we may judge as reflecting a magical or primitive view of religious life. The person may express depthful attachment to a particular religious book or devotional object. Regardless of our personal views on such matters, it is usually not wise to attempt to fix these attachments since, in the person's viewpoint, these attachments are not broken.

Conclusion

In the final analysis, the religious care of another person is primarily an art which requires the use of discernment rather than a science which insists on a rigorous application of mandated techniques. In our self-proclaimed postmodern age, with its increasing emphasis upon demonstrated results arising from treatment tactics applied to specific diagnostic entities, religious diagnosis may still seem to be too softly focused. Nevertheless, I believe Thomas Moore is correct when he urges "our work in psychology would change remarkably if we thought about it as ongoing care rather than as the quest for a cure. We might take the time to watch and listen as gradually it reveals the deeper mysteries lying within daily turmoil."[131]

This tension highlights a more fundamental philosophic division within both the religious and secular communities of care. It is the division between those who view care from a teleological viewpoint (where *facts* are pre-eminent), which tends to insist upon specific ends arrived at through specific means, and those who view care from an ontological viewpoint (where *values* are pre-eminent), which tends to perceive both the wounds of the person and the delivery of care as arising from the more fundamental nature of human existence. We must use this distinction to highlight the limitations and resources in varied approaches to care. But we only wound ourselves if we continue to judge one model of diagnosis and care by another model's standards of truth. As one author notes, "facts are not the universal domain of psychiatry as science and values the sole domain of religion as morality." The two realms "occupy the same country, the same landscape of meaning."[132] Perhaps a multi-axial system of religious diagnosis, used in tandem with a multi-axial system of clinical diagnosis, can underscore our common ground.

Chapter 11

Diagnosis and the Transcendent Function

Secular society is hungry for religious reality. We have begun remembering and attending to the Holy once more. Some have turned toward traditional religion in an attempt to find words appropriate enough to express the awe of photographs from the edge of the galaxy. Some have ventured into the spiritual dimensions of life because the secular therapies and weekend retreats have been unable to bring them true warmth and genuine healing. Some come without much connection to a historic faith community while others seem to be intent upon a journey beyond the confines of Westernized theology.

Whenever the aches of life compel us to seek religious counsel, there will need to be caregivers who are competent enough to begin hearing our pain and guiding us toward relief. While all religious traditions have resources for healing, a particular religion's strengths may not match the wounds of the person who stands before us. It behooves us as providers of care, whether religious or secular, to be aware of the resources within the wider religious community. We are clearly not the first ones to travel this road, even if our current generation's arrogance tempts us to believe that we are this special. But even more, we are called to direct people toward the manifestation of Greatness which will best restore them to wholeness. This means we must become aware of the limitations within our own circle of theology and piety. We must be honest enough to recognize the times when a particular brand of religious caring may not be the most efficacious for a person.

Foremost, those who provide for the religious well being of other persons must be comfortable with Mystery. Not just the "mysteries" of faith, as in "was Jesus really married?" or "how *did* Buddha actually sit all those years under the Bo tree?" We must bear witness to the Mystery beyond all our names, rites, doctrines and techniques. We must create and maintain a place in our culture for people to come, with their wounds and wonder, and stand in the presence of the God Who Looks For Us. We must preserve an arena where there can be dancing in joy for reconciliation and longing in faith for a mercy one cannot yet name.

The model of religious diagnosis presented in these pages attempts to take seriously our need to *name* our pain. Our distress does not usually fall from the sky fully formed. Our anguish has antecedents in our own behavior and the lives of many others who have acted upon us, not always with the most skill or the most benevolent of intentions. But we cannot fully name our wounds, for we cannot fully know the depths of our distress. This model of diagnosis also takes seriously the agnostic qualities inherent in the care of persons. Within the current environment of care, two areas of parallel concern seem important.

The Continuing Professionalization of Religious Care

Religious persons have been in the forefront of the care of persons from the dawn of recorded history.[133],[134] Religious diagnosis is not a new development. Religious rubrics for the human dilemmas may be innovative but they occur within a long and honored tradition of wise compassion. The clinical movement within the religious community is very new when compared against a healing tradition of 3,000 years. Yet the clinical movement is an important development, born of the necessity to integrate modern therapeutic techniques, contemporary psychologies and the archaic roots of healing ministry. The struggle with the necessity of viewing hurting persons solely within a pathological model is one which cries out for a fuller explication of the human condition.[135]

This has at least two implications for the task of religious diagnosis and those who offer care from a religious framework. One implication is the expectation that the religiously oriented clinician will be professionally trained, able to speak collegially and competently with a wide variety of care providers.

The recent proliferation in managed health care programs and state licensure requirements for providers of care will continue to impact the religiously oriented caregiver. The American Psychiatric Association (APA) has recently begun a new effort to detail "what is known and what is not known about the treatment of patients." Believing that "the psychiatric profession should take the lead in describing the best treatments and the range of appropriate treatments available to patients with mental illness," the APA hopes to have these guildlines available shortly and to update them every three to five years.[136]

Parish clergy may not be directly affected by these guildlines except as consumers of mental health services. But clinically oriented pastoral counselors, chaplains within medical institutions and other religiously oriented clinicians will be directly affected by these guildlines. We will be attending workshops to learn what these guidelines are and how to implement them in our care of persons.

Conversations with health insurance providers, social service agencies and the legal system will be done within the confines of this language. Diagnosis and treatment will be done within these standards. Our training programs, already struggling to retain the spiritual focus which is unique to our identity will have to spend added staff time insuring that new clinicians are familiar with these standards of care.[137] As I noted elsewhere, this is a teleological model of diagnosis and care. It is simply a part of the modern professional counseling landscape.[138, 139]

I am not suggesting that clergy or religious counselors in general lead a charge back into the Middle Ages. We must participate within the wider world of caregivers. There must continue to be ways to name and honor the ineffable within the person. We must provide them. We allow the secular clinical community to construct religious guildlines - or avoid including religion in the guidelines - at our mutual peril. Unfortunately, the religious clinical community is still struggling to answer two basic questions, if a recent issue of *The Journal of Pastoral Care*[140] provides any accurate picture of our discussion. The writers appear to be wrestling with these questions: 1) "what do you have to say about this case that the psychologist and social worker haven't already said?" and 2) "how can you describe a person's dilemma in a way that is intelligible to both the person and other professions?" While several articles in this issue affirm "a fundamental interdependency between psychological and spiritual processes taking place within persons,"[141] none of the writers present a model that practically unifies these areas. If religious counselors are struggling with how to speak to the psychiatric community, one writer notes the paucity of effort on the other side of this conversation, "religion rarely appears in the pages of psychiatry's text books." [142]

Religiously oriented care providers must find ways of documenting and communicating our healing approaches to the wider audiences of care providers.[143] We must find a language that does this, being clinically congruent and spiritually genuine. The *Dictionary of Pastoral Care* is an excellent step in this direction. Some state licensure exams include questions which invite licensees to consider how they would respond to a religiously oriented client. This is an important recognition by the secular clinical community of the significant role religion plays in the well being of a person. The hiring of a Research Coordinator by the American Association of Pastoral Counselors (AAPC), while a belated step is nevertheless another welcomed signal that clinical trained religious professionals intend to make their own contributions to the literature of human care more accessible to the research community. The days have long passed when a simple pastoral letter to a kindly judge or a finely tuned anecdote spoken to an anonymous case manager will insure the care of someone who has come to us for relief.

A second implication will be the sophistication of those who avail themselves of religious care. They will want care which is spiritually satisfying while being intellectually honest. Two early studies documented the significant role of religion in the wider world of mental health[144],[145] Little in the last thirty years has shaken these studies conclusions.[146] Instead, people have shown an increasing hunger for care which combines the unspeakable dimensions of the self along with the very recognizable maladies of body and mind. Thus there remains a need for care which has some ontological components.[147]

Some researchers, most notably Everett Worthington and Allen E. Bergin, have produced numerous studies outlining the behaviors and attitudes which people expect from religiously oriented counselors.[148] Worthington's research also describes what effective religiously oriented counselors *do.* It behooves providers of religious care to study this research and implement its conclusions with the same attentiveness they give psychiatrically developed guidelines for care. Other research shows rather clearly that if there is insufficient congruence between a counselor's and counseless' values and practices (theology and piety), the person receiving the care will choose someone else if offered the opportunity.[149]

This coincides with emerging research which documents less denominational fidelity among current religious persons. People increasingly seek out those congregations and pastors who are adept providers of care. In a nation hungry for humane, personal caring, the local pastor, rabbi, iman or other representative of the religious community can be a significant addition to the overall care we extend to one another. Thus when recently visiting both a Roman Catholic and a large evangelical congregation in Richmond, I was not surprised at all to see a well-appointed office for the Associate Pastor of Pastoral Care and Visitation, located adjacent to the receptionist's desk. Large congregations have offered these resources for years. Religious counseling agencies have sought financial support from clusters of faith groups to provide clinically trained religious persons to communities for years. Certainly a pastoral care center such as those operating on the Samaritan Center model, which stresses local congregational support, has much to commend it as we enter the next century.

In a related matter, denominations appear to be increasingly concerned about the psychological and spiritual health of all religious professionals. Faith groups have rightly insisted upon theological congruency and general standards for piety among its leadership for centuries. Now, with glaring revelations of clergy in all faith groups engaging in sexual predations there is a new awareness of the necessity for psychological screening of ministerial candidates. There is also a renewed recognition that once in ministry, religious professionals remain highly vulnerable to stress. It is increasingly obvious that people will no longer tolerate abuse by clergy under the guise that somehow the clergy's identity as "helping God" gives the right to immoral or abusive behavior. Stress reduction programs, support groups, and continuing education programs offered by denomination offices and area counseling agencies can support religious caregivers in their continued growth.

Coda: Others Who Are Not of this Vineyard

Our planet's religious resources are pluralistic. Those who provide religious care face a delicate task. We must become cognizant of, and conversant with, the broad outlines of these resources. Yet reducing these resources to a monodimensional piety devalues each religion's strengths. It also displays intellectual laziness and emotional infidelity. Buddha is not Jesus of Nazareth. Following the *tao* brings one to a place in the heart which the mystics may describe as unitive but which the ordinary person will experience as fundamentally distinct from the strictures of *Allah*.

It is not our initial task to provide people with a sophisticated religious education or transcultural religious exposure. It *is* our task as caregivers to offer people understandable care within the rubrics of faith, theology and piety which they can tolerate. Spiritual growth may happen, hopefully. We may even become a catalyst for a fully formed spiritual pilgrimage.

But we do people harm by misapplying religious resources we only vaguely understand in the same way we injure them by using psychological tools for which we have not received adequate training. This is a particularly pointed challenge at the interface of religious and secular care. Many secular care providers now offer mini-courses in spiritual healing and prayer. The rationale seems to be that since all people have some religious sentiment, all people -- certainly all professionally trained caregivers -- can translate their religious sentiment into religious care.

I take aspirins for occasional pain. But this does not qualify me to dispense them to others. It certainly does not make me a physician.

It is my perception that only as we continue to develop guidelines for adequate religious care, including a consistent language for diagnosis, will a consuming public make informed evaluations and choices about the religious care provided by many. It is with the hope of continuing the development of such a language that this model is offered to all who provide religiously oriented care, or who seek to integrate religious values into their clinical work. We have much to speak and reason about together. *Selah!*

Epilogue

My great-grandfather's hickory walking stick was rediscovered by our family only as I neared graduation from seminary. Not surprisingly, it fits my stature perfectly. It is as trustworthy a companion on the reflective strolls I take as the lightweight tent and sturdy ropes which accompany me on more arduous treks. All of these aids are necessary components to the simple healing task of walking in nature.

This is an exciting era in which to be a counselor. We have an increasingly universal clinical language that, in its present incarnation, reminds us repeatedly to use its categories as guides. The DSM-IV takes seriously the cultural, ethnic and religious considerations that influence the assessment of distress and guide the delivery of care. From well-formulated clinical studies we also have an increasing recognition of the power of religion to be efficacious in the care of persons.

As new cultures pour into this on-going experiment we call America, it is as often the religious leader who can tell the healing story, as it is the medical practitioner who can administer the curative medicine that assists in restoring a person's sense of well-being. These new cultures, with their demand for equity, call healers of all persuasions-sions to be cooperative rather than competitive with each other.

At the same time the excesses of managed care, or as some sources perceive, managed *cost* in the care of our fellow citizens has once again made us aware that there is more to getting well and staying healthy than receiving the correct procedure from the cheapest practitioner. We have begun reasserting that fundamental human dignity includes the opportunity for depthful relationships in which fundamental questions of meaning can be explored in an unhurried, non-coercive fashion.

We have begun reclaiming our souls as clinicians and as citizens. I can think of few things more exciting.

Donald D. Denton , Jr. - Ordinary Time, 1997

Notes

---

[1] Thomas C. Ogden, *Care of Souls in the Classic Tradition* (Philadelphia: Fortress Press, 1978), 54.

[2] David W. Augsburger, *Pastoral Counseling Across Cultures* (Philadelphia: The Westminster Press, 1986), 316.

[3] Dvorah Simon, *Handbook of Solution-Focused Brief Therapy*, Scott D. Miller, Mark A. Hubble, Barry L. Duncan (San Francisco: Jossey-Bass Publishers, 1996), 44.

[4] Paul Pruyser, *The Minister as Diagnostician* (Philadelphia: The Westminster Press, 1976), 61.

[5] Don S. Browning, *Religious Ethics and Pastoral Care* (Philadelphia: Fortress Press, 1983), 57.

[6] P. W. Pruyser, *Dictionary of Pastoral Care and Counseling*, 1990 ed., s.v. "Evaluation and Diagnosis, Religious," 371-373.

[7] Paul Ricoeur, *The Symbolism of Evil* (Boston: Beacon Press, 1967), 10-14.

8 Alcoholics Anonymous World Services, *The Big Book: Alcoholics Anonymous* (New York: Alcoholics Anonymous World Services, 1976), 64.

9Mark 5:3f.

10 Arthur Waley, *The Analects of Confucius* (New York: Random House, 1938), 97.

11 John L. Cox, *Psychiatry and Religion: Context, Consensus and Controversies*, Dinesh Bhugra (New York: Routledge, 1996), 158.

12 Paul Ricoeur, *The Symbolism of Evil* (Boston: Beacon Press, 1967), 74.

13Genesis 2:16-17.

14 Bernard Spilka, Ralph W. Hood, Richard L. Gorsuch, *The Psychology of Religion An Empirical Approach* (Englewood Cliffs: Prentice-Hall, Inc., 1985), 66.

15Genesis 3:10.

16 Don S. Browning, *Religious Ethics and Pastoral Care* (Philadelphia: Fortress Press, 1983), 18-30.

17 Don S. Browning, *Religious Ethics and Pastoral Care* (Philadelphia: Fortress Press, 1983), 54.

18 Edwin Herr and Spencer Niles, "The Values of Counseling: Three Domains," *Counseling and Values* 33 (1988): 4-16.

19W. D. Ross, *Ethics: Selections from Classical and Contemporary Writers*, Oliver A. Johnson (Chicago: Holt, Rinehart and Winston, 1965), 401.

[20]W. D. Ross, *Ethics: Selections from Classical and Contemporary Writers*, Oliver A. Johnson (Chicago: Holt, Rinehart and Winston, 1965), 402.

[21] Edith Hamilton, *Mythology* (New York: Little, Brown & Company, 1940), 88.

[22]Romans 12:19.

[23]Romans 1:18.

[24] James W. Fowler, *Becoming Adult, Becoming Christian* (San Francisco: Harper & Row, 1984), 50.

[25] Paul Ricoeur, *The Symbolism of Evil* (Boston: Beacon Press, 1967), 100.

[26] Nicolai Hartmann, *Ethics; Selections from Classical and Contemporary Writers*, Oliver A. Johnson (Chicago: Holt, Rinehart and Winston, 1965), 383.

[27] Nicolai Hartman, *Ethics: Selections from Classical and Contemporary Writers*, Oliver A. Johnson (Chicago: Holt, Rinehart and Winston, 1965), 394.

[28] Nicolai Hartmann, *Ethics: Selections from Classical and Contemporary Writers*, Oliver A. Johnson (Chicago: Holt, Rinehart and Winston, 1965), 392.

[29] Immanuel Kant, *Growndwork of the Metaphysic of Morals* (New York: Harper & Row, 1948), 13.

[30] James Gustafson, *Ethics from a Theocentric Perspective*, vol. 2 (Chicago: University of Chicago Press, 1984), 8-10.

[31]Matthew 22:37-39.

[32] Immanuel Kant, *Groundwork of the Metaphysic of Morals* (New York: Harper & Row, 1948), 88.

[33] Robert Lovinger, *Religion and Counseling: The Psychological Impact of Religious Belief* (New York: The Continuum Publishing Co., 1990), 91-139.

[34] Max L. Stackhouse, *Creeds, Society and Human Rights: Study in Three Cultures* (Grand Rapids, Michigan: William B. Eerdmans Publishing Co., 1984), 33.

[35] Don S. Browning, *Religious Ethics and Pastoral Care* (Philadelphia: Fortress Press, 1983), 55.

[36] James Gustafson, *Ethics from a Theocentric Perspective*, vol. 2 (Chicago: University of Chicago, 1984), 303-315.

[37] Exodus 20:3-17.

[38] Matthew 5:3-11, Luke 6:30-26.

[39] I Corinthians 13:4-7.

[40] Galatians 6:14-26, Colossians 3:8-17.

[41] "A Scout is trustworthy, loyal, helpful, friendly, courteous, kind, obedient, cheerful, thrifty, brave, clean and reverent."

[42] Aaron A. Beck, *et. al., Cognitive Therapy of Depression* (New York: The Guilford Press, 1979), 396.

[43] Acts of the Apostles 9:4.

[44] Dorothee Solle, *Suffering* (Philadelphia: Fortress Press, 1975), 73.

[45] I Corinthians 6:1-6.

[46] Dorothee Solle, *Suffering* (Philadelphia: Fortress Press, 1975), 73.

[47] Sheldon Zimberg, *The Clinical Management of Alcoholism* (New York: Brunner/Mazel, 1983), 120.

[48] James W. Fowler, *Stages of Faith: The Psychology of Human Development and the Quest for Meaning* (New York: Harper&Row, 1981), 274.

[49] 2 Corinthians 5:17.

[50] Merle R. Jordan, *Taking on the Gods: The Task of the Pastoral Counselor* (Nashville: Abingdon Press Press Press, 1986), 18.

[51] Ana-Maria Rizzuto, *Exploring Sacred Landscapes: Religious and Spiritual Experiences in Psychotherapy*, Mary Lou Randour (New York: Columbia University Press, 1993), 16f.

[52] Albert Ellis, "Rational-Emotive Therapy (RET) and Pastoral Counseling: A Reply to Richard Wessler," *The Personnel and Guidance Journal* 62 (1984): 266-267.

[53] Stephen Quackenbos, "Psychotherapy and Religion: Rapprochement or Antithesis?" *Journal of Counseling and Development* 65 (1986): 84.

[54] Howard Clinebell, *Basic Types of Pastoral Counseling* (Nashville: Abingdon Press Press Press Press, 1966), 118-19.

[55] Edith Hamilton, *Mythology* (New York: Little, Brown & Company, 1940), 54f.

[56] Peter Trachtenberg, *The Casanova Complex: Compulsive Lovers & Their Women* (New York: Poseidon Press, 1988), 28.

[57] Gordon Prange, *At Dawn We Slept: The Untold Story of Peral Harbor* (New York: Viking Press, 1981), 47.

[58] Kyle Johnson, "Theopathology: Concept, Assessment, Intervention," *The Journal of Pastoral Care* 45 (1991): 244-252.

[59] Ana-Maria Rizzuto, *Exploring Sacred Landscapes: Religious and Spiritual Experiences in Psychotherapy*, Mary Lou Randour (New York: Columbia University Press, 1993), 18.

[60] Ana-Maria Rizzuto, *Exploring Sacred Landscapes: Religious and Spiritual Experiences in Psychotherapy*, Mary Lou Randour (New York: Columbia University Press, 1993), 19f.

[61] John G. Gunderson, et. al., "The Phenomenological and Conceptual Interface Between Borderline Personality Disorder and PTSD," *The American Journal of Psychiatry* 150 (1993): 23.

[62] Tim Kochems, *Exploring Sacred Landscapes: Religious and Spiritual Experiences in Psychotherapy*, Mary Lou Randour (New York: Columbia University Press, 1993), 38.

[63] Robert Bork, *Slouching Toward Gomorrah: Modern Liberalism and American Decline* (New York: HarperCollins Publishers, Inc., 1996), 282.

[64] John McDargh, "Concluding Clinical Postscript" in *Exploring Sacred Landscapes: Religious and Spiritual Experiences in Psychotherapy*, Mary Lou Randour (New York: Columbia University Press, 1993), 178.

[65] Job 38:2-3.

[66] Job 42:2.

[67] Psalm 16:10.

[68] Howard Cooper, *Psychiatry and Religion: Context, Consensus and Controversies*, Dinesh Bhugra (New York: Routledge, 1996), 76.

[69] Howard Cooper, *Psychiatry and Religion: Context, Consensus and Controversies*, Dinesh Bhugra (New York: Routledge, 1996), 76f.

[70] Joseph Campbell, *The Masks of God: Primitive Mythology* (New York: Penguin Books, 1976), 59.

[71] Martha L. Rogers, "A Call for Discernment--Natural and Spiritual: An Introductory Editorial to a Special Issue on SRA," *Journal of Psychology and Theology* 20 (1992): 175-186.

[72] Ruth Hennesy, *Personal Bereavement and Its Effects on the Choice of Religious Vocation,* diss., Northwestern University, 1987 (Evanston: Northwestern University Press, 1987), 247.

[73] Donald D. Denton, "The Warrior's Prayer: Combat Experience, Vocational Choice and Depth Relationships Among Vietnam Veterans Who Become Clergy," *The Journal of Pastoral Care* 45 (1991): 107-116.

[74] Paul Tillich, *Systematic Theology*, vol. Vol. 1 (Chicago: University of Chicago Press, 1951), Pages.

[75] Ana-Maria Rizzuto, *Exploring Sacred Landscapes: Religious and Spiritual Experiences in Psychotherapy*, Mary Lou Randour (New York: Columbia University Press, 1993), 26.

[76] Genesis 3:22-23.

[77] Peter A. Bertocci, *The Person God Is* (New York: Humanities Press, 1970), 19.

[78] Genesis 3:8.

[79] Exodus 19:3.

[80] Genesis 3:14-19.

[81] Merle R. Jordan, *Taking on the Gods: The Task of the Pastoral Counselor* (Nashville: Abingdon, 1986), 18.

116   *Religious Diagnosis in a Secular Society*

82 Donald D. Denton, *Combat Experience, Vocational Choice and Depth Relationships Among Vietnam Veteran Who Become Clergy,* diss., Garrett-Evangelical Theological Seminary, 1990 (Evanston: Garrett-Evangelical Theological Seminary, 1990), 10.

83 Joseph Campbell, *The Masks of God: Primitive Mythology* (New York: Penguin Press, 1976), 135.

84 Edward P. Wimberly, *Prayer in Pastoral Counseling:Suffering, Healing and Discernment* (Louisville: Westminster/John Knox Press, 1990), 11.

85Romans 6:15-23.

86I Kings 19:12, Ezekiel 1:4f.

87Luke 11:26.

88Romans 8:39.

892 Cor. 12:8.

902 Cor. 3:17.

91 Anton T. Boisen, *The Exploration of the Inner World: A Study of Mental Disorder and Religious Experience* (Philadelphia: University of Pennsylvania Press, 1936), 53.

92 St. Anselm, *The Ontological Argument from St. Anselm to Contemporary Philosophers,* Alvin Plantinga (New York: Anchor Books, 1965), 4.

93 Paul Ricoeur, *The Symbolism of Evil* (Boston: Beacon Press, 1967), 33.

94Genesis 4:10-15.

[95] B. B. McKinney, Music Editor, *The Broadman Hymnal*, 1940 ed., s.v. "Love Lifted Me," 352.

[96] Paul Ricoeur, *The Symbolism of Evil* (Boston: Beacon Press, 1967), 35.

[97] Paul Ricoeur, *The Symbolism of Evil* (Boston: Beacon Press, 1967), 55.

[98] *Diagnostic and Statistical Manual*, IV ed., s.v. "Personality Disorders," 629-30.

[99] John 4:1-26. The entire pericope illustrates pastoral conversation where healing symbol is embodied in presence of counselor.

[100] Thomas Merton, *Contemplative Prayer* (New York: Doubleday & Company, Inc., 1969), 24.

[101] I Kings 19:13.

[102] Paul Ricoeur, *The Symbolism of Evil* (Boston: Beacon Press, 1967), 36.

[103] Genesis 4:14.

[104] Matthew 26:40.

[105] Donald D. Denton, "Empathy and Archetype: The Structure of Healing," *The Journal of Pastoral Care* 47 (1992): 235f.

[106] Thomas Merton, *Contemplative Prayer* (New York: Doubleday & Company, Inc., 1969), 100.

[107] Mary Louise Bringle, "Soul-Dye and Salt: Integrating Spiritual and Medical Understanding," *The Journal of Pastoral Care* 50 (1996): 330.

[108] Mary Louise Bringle, "Soul-Dye and Salt: Integrating Spiritual and Medical Understanding," *The Journal of Pastoral Care* 50 (1996): 332.

[109] Luke 15:24.

[110] John 4:29.

[111] Psalm 130.

[112] Mark Sutherland, *Psychiatry and Religion: Context, Consensus and Controversies*, Dinesh Bhugra (New York: Routledge, 1996), 228.

[113] Howard L. Rice, *Reformed Spirituality: An Introduction for Believers* (Louisville: Westminster/John Knox Press, 1991), 37f.

[114] This is a typical pastoral prayer I use in worship.

[115] David W. Augsberger, *Pastoral Counseling Across Cultures* (Philadelphia: The Westminster Press, 1986), 33.

[116] Donald D. Denton, "Empathy and Archetype: The Structure of Healing," *The Journal of Pastoral Care* 47 (1992): 235.

[117] Joseph Lichtenberg, *Empathy II* (New York: Brunner/Mazel, 1985), 272-73.

[118] David W. Augsberger, *Pastoral Counseling Across Cultures* (Philadelphia: The Westminster Press, 1986), 368.

[119] Isaiah 40:31.

[120] Anton T. Boisen, *The Exploration of the Inner World: A Study of Mental Disorder and Religious Experience* (Philadelphia: University of Pennsylvania Press, 1936), 214f.

[121] K. W. M. Fulford, *Psychiatry and Religion: Context, Consensus and Controversies*, Dinesh Bhugra (New York: Routledge, 1996), 18.

122 Ludwig Wittgenstein, *Tractatus Logico-Phuilosophicus*, D. F. Pears & B. F. McGinness, 2 ed. (London: Routledge & Kegan Paul, 1961), 3.

123 Job 42:3.

124 John R. Peteet, "Religious Issues Presented by Cancer Patients Seen in Psychiatric Consultation," *Journal of Psychosocial Oncology* 3/1 (1985): 57-59.

125 John R. Peteet, "Religious Issues Presented by Cancer Patients Seen in Psychiatric Consultation," *Journal of Psychosocial Oncology* 31/1(1985):57-59.

126 John Foskett, *Psychiatry and Religion: Context, Consensus and Controversies*, Dinesh Bhugra (New York: Routledge, 1996), 51.

127 John Foskett, *Psychiatry and Religion: Context, Consensus and Controversies*, Dinesh Bhugra (New York: Routledge, 1996), 53.

128 Thomas Moore, *Care of the Soul* (New York: HarperCollins Publishers, 1994), 5.

129 Thomas Moore, *Care of the Soul* (New York: HarperCollins Publishers, 1994), 5.

130 James W. Fowler, *Stages of Faith: The Psychology of Human Development and the Quest for Meaning* (New York: Harper & Row, 1981), 51.

131 Thomas Moore, *Care of the Soul* (New York: HarperCollins Publishers, 1994), 19.

132 K. W. M. Fulford, "Religion and Psychiatry: Extending the Limits of Tolerance" in *Psychiatry and Religion: Context, Consensus and Controversies*, Dinesh Bhurgra (New York: Routledge, 1996), 5.

[133] Dinesh Bhugra, *Psychiatry and Religion: Context, Consensus and Controversies*, Dinesh Bhugra (New York: Routledge, 1996), 1.

[134]Genesis 4:15.

[135] Dvorah Simon, *Solution Focused Brief Therapy*, Scott D. Miller, Mark A. Hubble, Barry L. Duncan (San Francisco: Jossey-Bass Publishers, 1996), 57.

[136] Deborah Zarin, et. al., "Practice Guidelines," *The American Journal of Psychiatry* 150 (1993): 2.

[137] Marvin Gardner, "Integrating the Pastoral Dimension into Pastoral Counselor Training Programs," *The Journal of Pastoral Care* 47 (1993): 63.

[138] Donald D. Denton, "Guilt, Betrayal and Stain: A Prolegomena to Multiaxial Pastoral Diagnosis," *The Journal of Pastoral Care* 47 (1993): 15.

[139] Dvorah Simon, *Handbook of Solution-Focused Brief Therapy*, Scott D. Miller, Mark A. Hubble, Barry L. Duncan (San Francisco: Jossey-Bass, Inc., 1996), 57.

[140] This issue contains articles which appear   as though the movement is still wrestling with theoretical questions more appropriate to a new movement rather than a discipline that has been practiced for 50 years.

[141] Robert B. Kosek, "The Contribution of Object Relations Theory in Pastoral Counseling," *The Journal of Pastoral Care* 50/4 (1996): 381.

[142] John Foskett, *Psychiatry and Religion: Context, Consensus and Controversies*, Dinesh Bhugra (New York: Routledge, 1996), 51.

[143] Rob A. Ruff, ""Leaving Footprints": The Practice and Benefits of Hospital Chaplains Documenting Pastoral Care Activity in Patients' Medical Records," *The Journal of Pastoral Care* 50/4 (1996): 383-391.

[144] R. V. McCann, *The Churches and Mental Health* (New York: Basic Books, 1962), Pages.

[145] G. Gurin, et. al., *Americans View Their Mental Health* (New York: Basic Books, 1960), Pages.

[146] Stephen Quackenbos, et. al., "Psychotherapy and Religion: Rapprochement or Antithesis?" *Journal of Counseling and Development* 65 (1986): 84.

[147] Donald D. Denton, "Guilt, Betrayal and Stain: A Prolegomena to Multiaxial Pastoral Diagnosis," *The Journal of Pastoral Care* 47 (1993): 15.

[148] Allen E. Bergin, "Three Contributions of a Spiritual Perspective to Counseling, Psychotherapy and Behavior Change," *Counseling and Values* 33 (1988): 21-31.

[149] Edwin Herr and Spencer Niles, "The Values of Counseling: Three Domains," *Counseling and Values* 33 (1988): 5-10.

Bibliography

Ahlskog, Gary. "The Paradox of Pastoral Psychotherapy." *The Journal of Pastoral Care* 49(2).

American Psychiatric Association. *Diagnostic and Statistical Manual,* Fourth Edition. Washington, D. C.: 1994.

Andreasen, Nancy C. "Body and Soul." *The American Journal of Psychiatry* 153(1996):589-590.

Ashbrook, James B. "The Complex Clarity of Pastoral Therapy: The Perspective of a Pioneer." *The Journal of Pastoral Care* 43(1986).

-------------------- *The Human Mind and the Mind of* God: *The Theological Promise of Brain Research.* University Press of America: Lanham, M. D., 1984.

Augsburger, David W. *Pastoral Counseling Across Cultures.* The Westminster Press: Philadelphia, PA, 1986.

Beck, Aaron A. et. al. *Cognitive Therapy of Depression.* New York: The Guilford Press, 1979.

Bergin, Allen E. "Three Contributions of a Spiritual Perspective to Counseling, Psychotherapy and Behavior Change." *Counseling and Values* 33(1988): 21-31.

Bertocci, Peter A. *The Person God Is.* New York: Humanities Press, 1970.

Bhugra, Dinesh, ed. *Psychiatry and Religion: Context, Consensus and Controversies.* New York: Routledge, 1996.

Boisen, Anton T. *The Exploration of the Inner World: A Study of Mental Disorder and Religious Experience.* Philadelphia, PA: University of Pennsylvania Press, 1936.

Bringle, Mary Louise. "Soul-Dye and Salt: Integrating Spiritual and Medical Understanding." *The Journal of Pastoral Care* 50(1996): 329-339.

Browning, Don S. *Religious Ethics and Pastoral Care.* Philadelphia, PA: Fortress Press, 1983.

Campbell, Joseph. *The Masks of God: Primitive Mythology.* New York: Penguin Books, 1976.

123

Clinebell, Howard. *Basic Types of Pastoral Care & Counseling.*
    Nashville, TN: Abingdon Press, 1966.
Denton, Donald D. "Guilt, Betrayal and Stain: A Prolegomena to
    Multiaxial Pastoral Diagnosis." *The Journal of Pastoral Care*
    47(1993).
-------------------------- "Empathy and Archetype: The Structure of
    Healing." *The Journal of Pastoral Care* 47(1992).
-------------------------- "The Warrior's Prayer: Combat Experience,
    Vocational Choice and Depth Relationships Among Vietnam
    Veterans Who Become Clergy." *The Journal of   Pastoral
    Care* 45 (1991): 107-116.
-------------------------- "War and Its Aftermath: Theological Resources
    for Preaching and Pastoral Care." *Lectionary Homiletics.*
    Vol. 2, No. 6 (May, 1990).
Ellis, Albert. "Rational-Emotive Therapy (RET) and Pastoral
    Counseling: A Reply to Richard Wessler." *The
    Personnel and Guidance Journal* 62(1984): 266-267.
Fisher, Bruce. "The Process of Healing Shame."*Alcoholism Treatment
    Quarterly* 4(1987): 25-38.
Fowler, James W. *Becoming Adult, Becoming Christian.* San
    Francisco: Harper & Row, 1984.
-------------------------- *Stages of Faith: The Psychology of Human
    Development and the Quest for Meaning.* New   York:
    Harper & Row, 1981.
Gardner, Marvin. "Integrating the Pastoral Dimension into Pastoral
    Counseling Training Programs." *The Journal of
    PastoralCare* 47(1993): 56-64.
Gerkin, Charles V. *The Living Human Document: Re-Visioning
    Pastoral Counseling in a Hermeneutical Mode.* Nashville:
    Abingdon Press, 1984.
Godin, Andre. *The Psychological Dynamics of Religious Experience.*
    Birmingham, AL: Religious Education Press, 1985.
Gunderson, John G. *et. al.* "The Phenomenological and Conceptual
    Interface Between Borderline Personality Disorder and
    PTSD." *The American Journal of Psychiatry* 150(1993): 19-
    29.
Gurin, G., *et. al. Americans View Their Mental Health.* New York:
    Basic Books, 1960.

Gustafson, James. *Ethics from a Theocentric Perspective.* Vol. 1 and 2. Chicago: University of Chicago Press, 1981.

Hamilton, Edith. *Mythology.* New York: Little, Brown &Company, 1940.

Ruth Hennesy, "Personal Bereavement and Its Effects on the Choice of Religious Vocation" (Ph.D. diss., Northwestern University, 1987).

Herr, Edwin and Niles, Spencer. "The Values of Counseling: Three Domains." *Counseling and Values* 33(1988):4-16.

Hunter, Rodney J., General Editor. *Dictionary of Pastoral Care.* Nashville: Abingdon Press, 1987.

Ivy, Steven S. "A Model for Pastoral Assessment." *The Journal of Pastoral Care* 49(1987): 329-340.

Johnson, Kyle. "Theopathology: Concept, Assessment, Intervention." *The Journal of Pastoral Care* 45 (1991): 244-252.

Johnson, Oliver A. *Ethics: Selections from Classical and Contemporary Writers.* Chicago: Holt, Rinehart and Winston, 1965.

Jordan, Merle R. *Taking on the Gods: The Task of the Pastoral Counselor.* Nashville: Abingdon, 1986.

Jacobi, Jolande. *Complex, Archetype, Symbol in the Psychology of C. G. Jung.* New York: Princeton University Press, 1959.

Kant, Immanuel. *Groundwork of the Metaphysic of Morals.* New York: Harper & Row, 1948.

Kohut, Heinz. *How Does Analysis Cure?* Chicago: University of Chicago Press, 1984.

Lichtenberg, Joseph. *Empathy II.* New York: Brunner/Mazel, 1985.

Lovinger, Robert J. *Religion and Counseling: The Psychological Impact of Religious Belief.* New York: The Continuum Publishing Co., 1990.

Marsella, Anthony J., et. al. eds. *Culture and Self: Asian and Western Perspectives.* New York: Tavistock Publications, 1985.

Marston, Robert. "Experiencing the Presence of God During Times of Need: A Case Study." *The Journal of Pastoral Care* 44(1990): 258-264.

McCann, R. V. *The Churches and Mental Health.* New York: Basic Books, 1962.

Merton, Thomas. *Contemplative Prayer.* Garden City, NJ: Doubleday & Company, Inc., 1969.

Miller, Scott D., Hubble, Mark A., Duncan, Barry L., eds. *Handbook of Solution-Focused Brief Therapy.* San Francisco: Jossey-Bass Publishers, 1996.

Moore, Thomas. *Care of the Soul.* New York: HarperCollins, 1992

New York International Bible Society. *New International Version of the Holy Bible.* East Brunswick, NJ: 1978.

Oden, Thomas C. *Care of Souls in the Classic Tradition.* Philadelphia: Fortress Press, 1978.

Patton, John. *Pastoral Counseling: A Ministry of the Church.* Nashville: Abingdon Press, 1983.

Peteet, John R. "Religious Issues Presented by Cancer Patients Seen in Psychiatric Consultation." *Journal of Psychosocial Oncology* 3(1985):53-66.

Plantinga, Alvin, ed. *The Ontological Argument from St. Anselm to Contemporary Philosophers.* New York: Anchor Books, 1965.

Prange, Gordon. *At Dawn We Slept: The Untold Story of Pearl Harbor.* New York: Viking Press, 1981.

Pruyser, Paul. *The Minister as Diagnostician.* Philadelphia: Westminster Press, 1976.

Quackenbos, Stephen, *et. al.* "Psychotherapy and Religion: Rapprochement or Antithesis?" *Journal of Counseling and Development* 65(1986):82-85.

Randour, Mary Lou, ed. *Exploring Sacred Landscapes: Religious Experiences in Psychotherapy.* New York, Columbia University Press, 1993.

Rice, Howard L. *Reformed Spirituality: An Introduction for Believers.* Louisville, Kentucky: Westminster/John Knox Press, 1991.

Ricoeur, Paul. *The Symbolism of Evil.* Boston: Beacon Press, 1967.

Rogers, Martha L. "A Call for Discernment--Natural and Spiritual: An Introductory Editorial to a Special Issue on SRA." *Journal of Psychology and Theology*   20(1992):175-186.

Ross, W. D. *Foundations of Ethics.* Oxford: Clarendon Press, 1939.

Ruff, Rob A. " ' Leaving Footprints' : The Practice and Benefits of Hospital Chaplains Documenting Pastoral Care Activity in Patients' Medical Records." *The Journal of Pastoral Care* 50/4(1996): 383-391.

Schlauch, Chris R. "Defining Pastoral Psychotherapy II." *The Journal of Pastoral Care* 41(1986):319-327

Spilka, Bernard, et. al. *The Psychology of Religion: An Empirical Approach.* Englewood Cliffs, NJ: Prentice-Hall, 1985.

Soelle, Dorothee. *Suffering.* Philadelphia: Fortress Press, 1975.

Stackhouse, Max L. *Creeds, Society and Human Rights: A Study in Three Cultures.* Grand Rapids, Michigan: William B. Eerdmans Publishing Co., 1984.

Tillich, Paul. *Systematic Theology,* Vol. 1. Chicago: University of Chicago Press, 1951.

Townsend, Loren. "Creative Theological Imagining: A Method for Pastoral Counseling." *The Journal of Pastoral Care* 50(1996):349-363.

Tractenberg, Peter. *The Casanova Complex: Compulsive Lovers and Their Women.* New York: Posidon Press, 1988.

Waley, Arthur. *The Analects of Confucius.* New York: Random House, 1938.

Webb, Linda J., et.al. *DSM-III Training Guide.* New York: Brunner/Mazel, 1981.

Wessler, Richard L. "A Bridge Too Far: Incompatibilities of Rational-Emotive Therapy and Pastoral Counseling." *The Personnel and Guidance Journal* 62(1984):264-266.

Wimberly, Edward P. *Prayer in Pastoral Counseling: Suffering, Healing and Discernment.* Louisville: Westminster/John Knox Press, 1990.

------------------------- *African American Pastoral Care.* Nashville, Tennessee: Abdingdon Press, 1991.

Wittgenstein, Ludwig. *Tractatus Logico-Philosophicus, 2nd.* London: Routledge & Kegan Paul, Ltd., 1961.

Worthington, Everett L. "Religious Counseling: A Review of Published Empirical Research." *Journal of Counseling and Development* 64(1986): 421-431.

Zarin, Deborah, et. al. "Practice Guidelines." *The American Journal of Psychiatry* 150(1993):2

Zimberg, Sheldon. *The Clinical Management of Alcoholism.* New York: Brunner/Mazel, 1983.

Index